1994 EDITION

The TRAVEL TRAINING WORKBOOK

Section Six
General Review and Sales Techniques

Claudine Dervaes

ISBN 0-933143-39-7   Section Six: General Review and
                     Sales Techniques

Other materials available from Solitaire Publishing:

ISBN 0-933143-46-X   The Travel Training Workbook set
ISBN 0-933143-44-3   Section One: Introduction to
                     Travel and Geography
ISBN 0-933143-38-9   Section Two: Domestic Travel and
                     Ticketing
ISBN 0-933143-36-2   Section Three: Supplemental Sales -
                     Hotels, Car Rentals, Packages,
                     Tours, Motorcoach and Rail
ISBN 0-933143-35-4   Section Four: International Travel
ISBN 0-933143-37-0   Section Five: Cruises

ISBN 0-933143-45-1   The Travel Dictionary
ISBN 0-933143-40-0   Map Transparencies Set
ISBN 0-933143-41-9   ARC Forms Transparencies Set
ISBN 0-933143-42-7   Training Specifics Transparencies Set
ISBN 0-933143-07-9   TEACHING TRAVEL: A Handbook for the
                     Educator

The author-publisher would like to thank John Stuart
Hunter for graphics and display work and Ray Endrizzi
for editing assistance.

TABLE OF CONTENTS

PREFACE

The <u>Travel</u> <u>Training</u> <u>Workbook</u> is designed to teach basic travel skills. It is divided into six sections:

Section One: Introduction to Travel and Geography

Section Two: Domestic Travel and Ticketing (with Travel Agency Computerization supplement)

Section Three: Supplemental Sales - Hotels and Car Rentals, Packages and Tours, Motorcoach and Rail

Section Four: International Travel

Section Five: Cruises

Section Six: General Review and Sales Techniques

SECTION SIX
General Review and Sales Techniques

General Review provides tests from all the previous sections of The <u>Travel</u> <u>Training</u> <u>Workbook</u>. This area also contains Travel Agency Proficiency and References/Resources Tests, which are useful for evaluating and improving the skills of travel industry employees.

Sales Techniques will guide the reader to success, with its in-depth examination of sales details and situations, listening skills, telephone courtesy, and techniques for handling complaints.

Under **Making Reservations** all types of forms and sample calls are provided, along with role-play activities and evaluations.

The **Psychology of Selling** is followed by **Marketing and Specialty Sales**, where guidelines and helpful forms on group travel, outside sales, and meeting planning are presented.

The **Business Communications** area exhibits sample forms, business writing skills, and sample correspondence.

Agency and Management Communications covers key items such as familiarization trip reports, cruise ship evaluations, employee evaluations, and travel agency filing procedures.

Job Search provides the details of preparing a resume, interview techniques, and other job taking hints. Some positions in travel, practical tips for the employer, and time and stress management finalize this section.

This workbook has been written to encourage and enhance profession-alism in the travel industry. As a purchaser you will be notified of revisions as they are accumulated.

MATCH THE INDUSTRY ASSOCIATIONS WITH THEIR FUNCTIONS/RESPONSIBILITIES

1. _____FAA
2. _____DOT
3. _____ARC
4. _____WTO
5. _____FMC
6. _____ARTA
7. _____ASTA
8. _____CLIA
9. _____IATAN
10. _____ICC

A. GIVING TOURISM ITS IMPORTANCE, STRENGTHENING INTERNATIONAL COOPERATION

B. APPOINTS TRAVEL AGENCIES, ACTS AS A CLEARING-HOUSE FOR TICKETS

C. REGULATORY AGENCY ON STEAMSHIP OPERATIONS, FOREIGN AND DOMESTIC OFFSHORE COMMERCE

D. DEPARTMENT OF THE GOVERNMENT THAT HANDLES CONSUMER AFFAIRS AND PROTECTION REGARDING AIRLINE TRAVEL OPERATIONS AND TRANSPORTATION

E. GOVERNMENT AGENCY THAT PROMOTES CIVIL AVIATION, TESTS AND LICENSES PILOTS, SETS SAFETY STAND-ARDS FOR AIRCRAFT, AIRPORTS, ETC.

F. PROMOTES CRUISES, WITH TRAINING MATERIALS, SHIP PROFILES, SEMINARS

G. ASSOCIATION OF INTERNATIONAL AIRLINES THAT PROMOTES STANDARD OPERATIONS AND UNIFORMITY OF PROCEDURES, FARES, ETC.

H. ONE OF THE LARGEST TRAVEL ORGANIZATIONS, ITS MEMBERSHIP IS COMPRISED OF TRAVEL AGENCIES, AIRLINES, TOUR OPERATORS, AND MANY OTHER COMPANIES

I. TRAVEL ASSOCIATION OF AMERICAN RETAIL TRAVEL AGENTS

J. COMMISSION REGULATING INTERSTATE COMMERCE

Note: These are just some of the many associations and organizations of the travel industry. Other major associations include the AH & MA (American Hotel and Motel Association), PATA (Pacific Area Travel Association), USTOA (United States Tour Operators Association), NTA (National Tour Association), and TIA (Travel Industry Association of America). A more complete list is given in **The Travel Dictionary**, available from Solitaire Publishing.

2

THE 24 HOUR CLOCK AND GENERAL GEOGRAPHY REVIEW

Convert into AM or PM

1. 0010 = _____

2. 1752 = _____

3. 1345 = _____

4. 0532 = _____

5. 1421 = _____

Convert into 24 HOUR CLOCK

6. 10:12 AM = _____

7. 12:20 PM = _____

8. 9:15 AM = _____

9. 8:45 PM = _____

10. 6:20 AM = _____

MATCH THE COUNTRIES TO THEIR CONTINENT:

11. _____ Morocco
12. _____ Mexico
13. _____ Indonesia
14. _____ Albania
15. _____ Philippines
16. _____ Venezuela
17. _____ Luxembourg
18. _____ Egypt

A. NORTH AMERICA
B. SOUTH AMERICA
C. EUROPE
D. AFRICA
E. ASIA
F. AUSTRALIA
G. ANTARCTICA

MATCH THE ISLANDS TO THE OCEANS IN WHICH THEY ARE LOCATED:

19. _____ Bermuda
20. _____ Galapagos
21. _____ Seychelles
22. _____ Canary
23. _____ Maldive Is.

A. ATLANTIC OCEAN
B. PACIFIC OCEAN
C. INDIAN OCEAN
D. ARCTIC OCEAN

MATCH THE PLACE OF INTEREST TO THE APPROPRIATE COUNTRY:

24. _____ Ayers Rock
25. _____ Taj Mahal
26. _____ Machu Picchu
27. _____ Sugarloaf Mountain
28. _____ Notre Dame Cathedral
29. _____ Neuchwanstein Castle
30. _____ Anne Hathaway's Cottage
31. _____ Xian Statues
32. _____ Aswan Dam
33. _____ Blue Mosque

A. FRANCE
B. TURKEY
C. CHINA
D. ENGLAND
E. GERMANY
F. EGYPT
G. AUSTRALIA
H. INDIA
I. PERU
J. BRAZIL

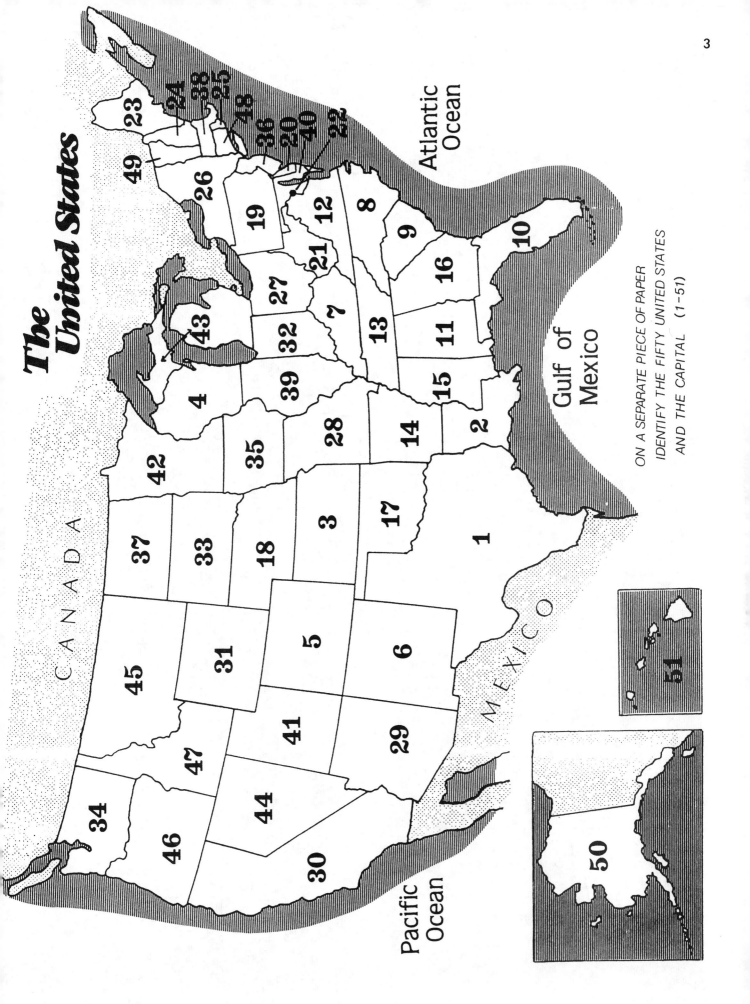

The United States

3

Atlantic Ocean

Gulf of Mexico

Pacific Ocean

CANADA

MEXICO

ON A SEPARATE PIECE OF PAPER
IDENTIFY THE FIFTY UNITED STATES
AND THE CAPITAL (1-51)

4

IDENTIFY THE ISLANDS
AND CITIES   (1-20)

8

1

9

17

13 2

20

19

16

15

3

14

4

Pacific
Ocean

18

5

10

Hawaii

6

11

12

7

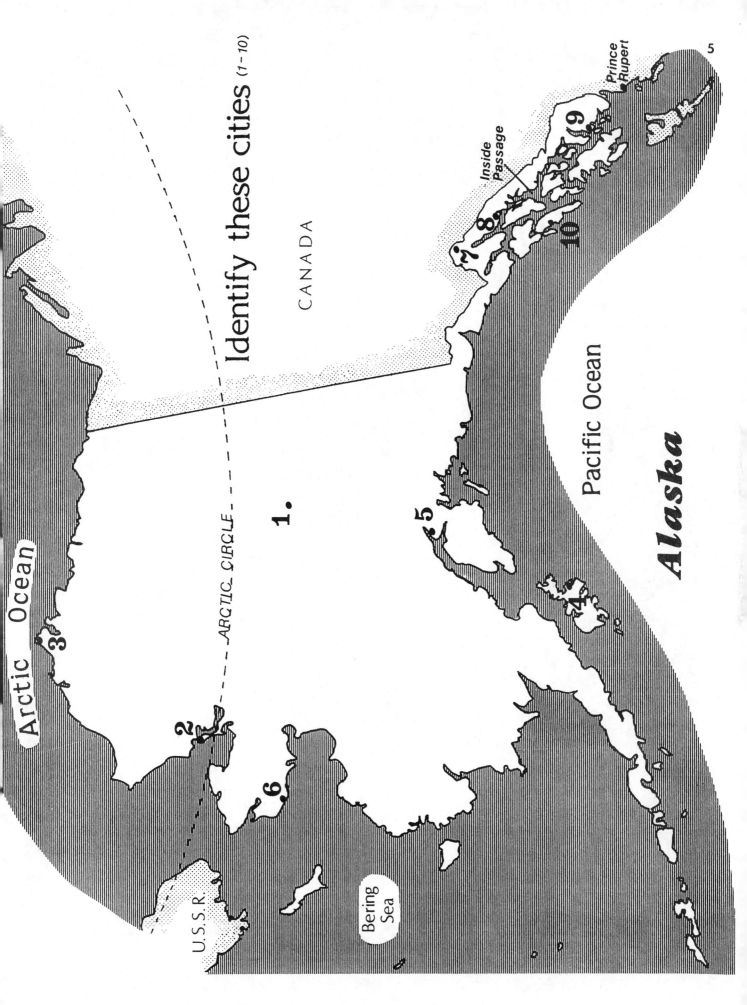

Identify these cities (1-10)

CANADA

Arctic Ocean

ARCTIC CIRCLE

U.S.S.R.

Bering
Sea

Pacific Ocean

Alaska

Inside
Passage

Prince
Rupert

5

1.

2

3

4

5

6

7

8

9

10

6

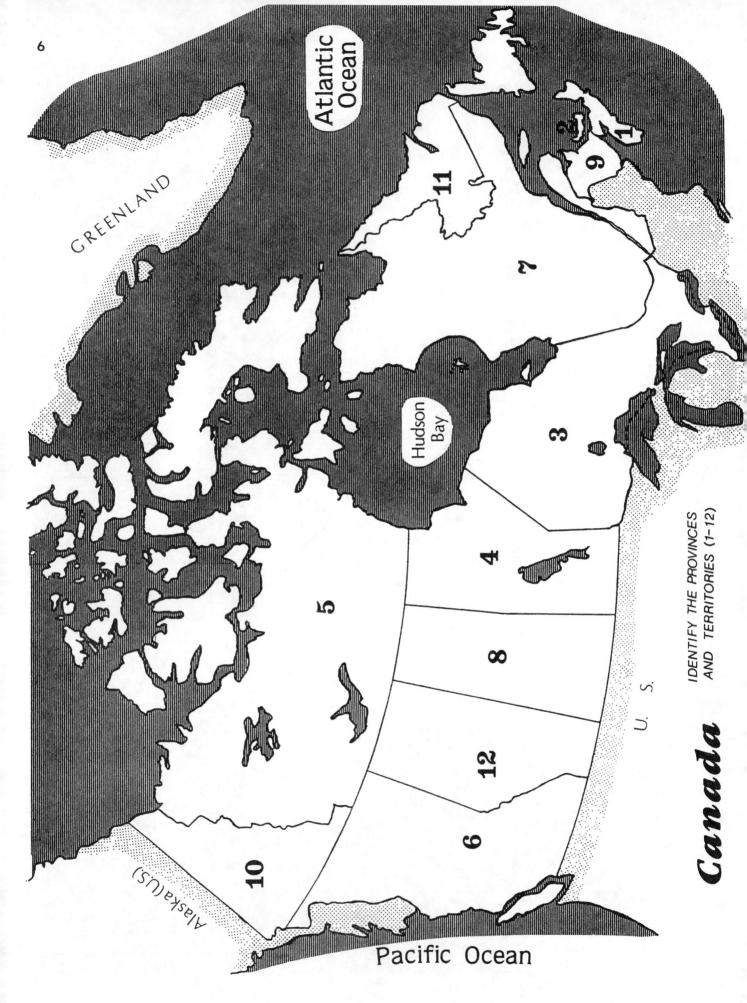

Atlantic Ocean

GREENLAND

Hudson Bay

Pacific Ocean

Alaska (U.S.)

U. S.

Canada

IDENTIFY THE PROVINCES AND TERRITORIES (1-12)

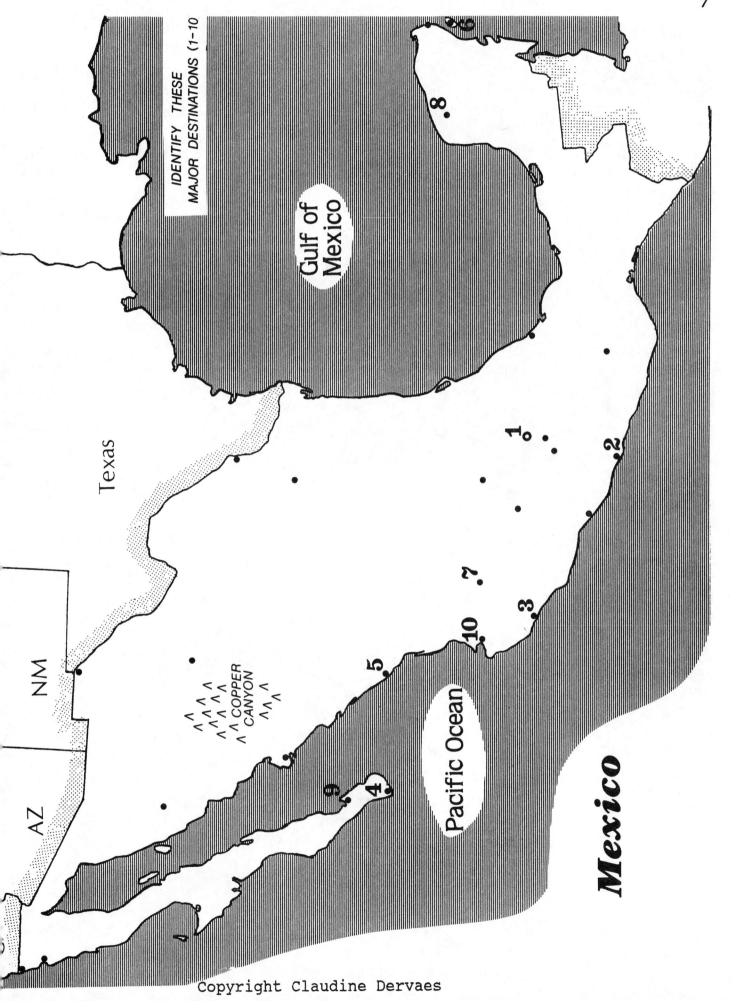

IDENTIFY THESE
MAJOR DESTINATIONS (1-10)

Gulf of
Mexico

Texas

NM

AZ

∧ ∧
∧ ∧ ∧
∧ ∧ ∧ ∧
∧ ∧ COPPER
∧ CANYON
∧ ∧ ∧
∧ ∧

Pacific Ocean

Mexico

8

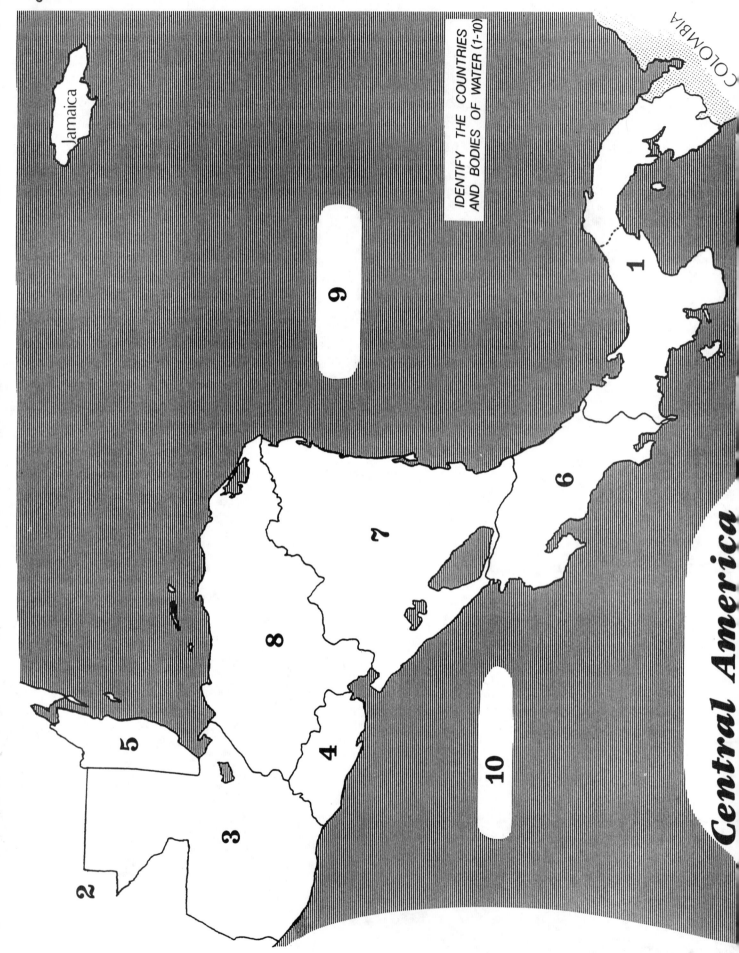

COLOMBIA

IDENTIFY THE COUNTRIES
AND BODIES OF WATER (1-10)

Jamaica

Central America

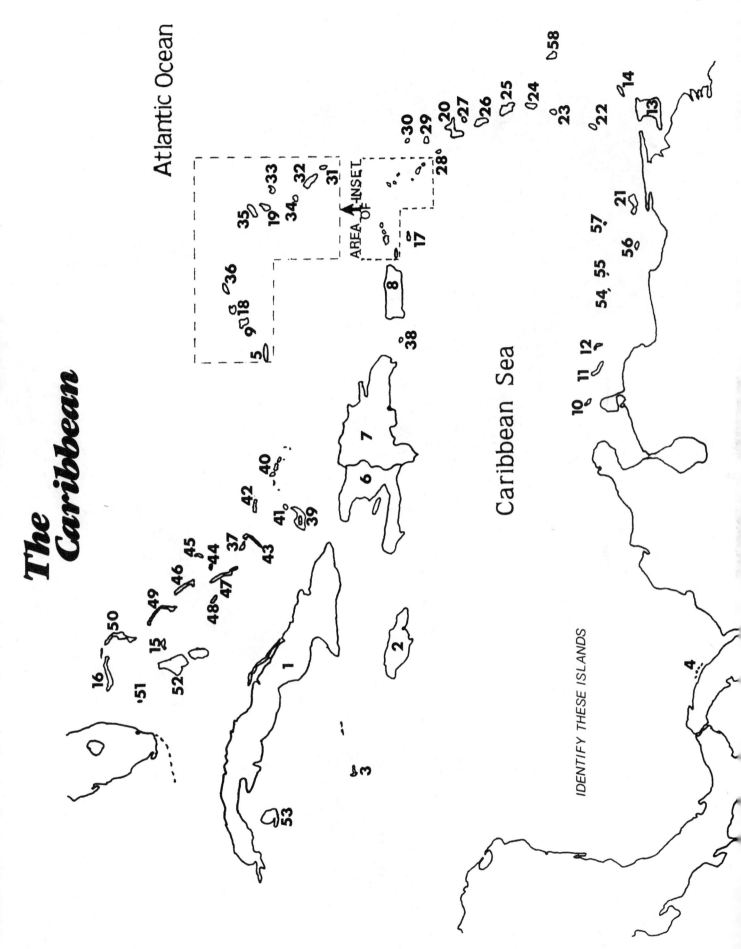

The Caribbean

Atlantic Ocean

Caribbean Sea

AREA OF INSET

IDENTIFY THESE ISLANDS

9

SOUTH AMERICA

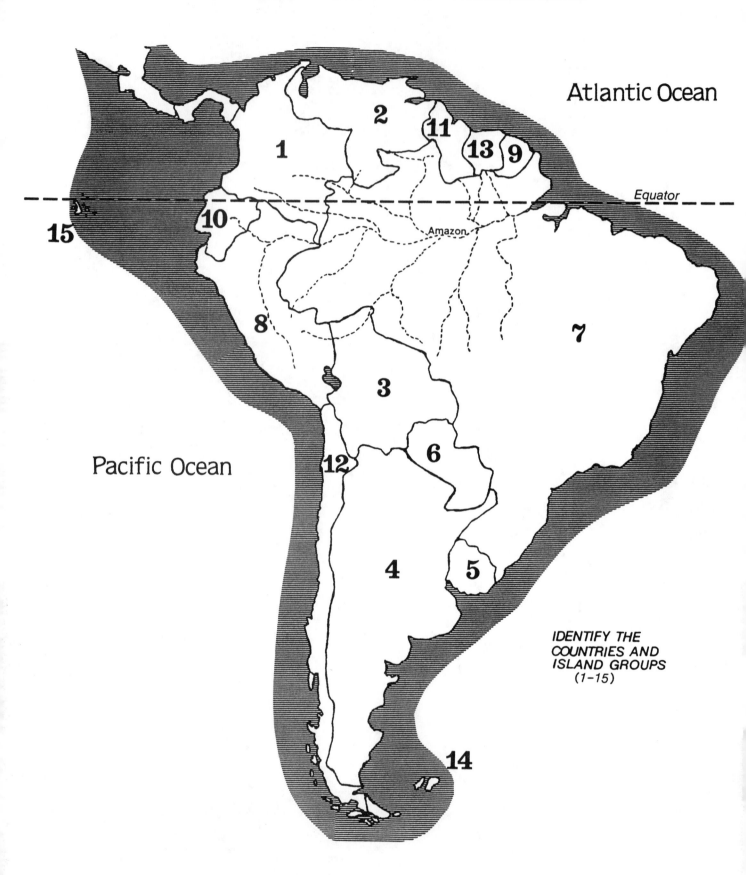

Atlantic Ocean

2

11

13 9

1

Equator

10

15

Amazon

8

Pacific Ocean

7

3

6

12

IDENTIFY THE
COUNTRIES AND
ISLAND GROUPS
(1-15)

4

5

14

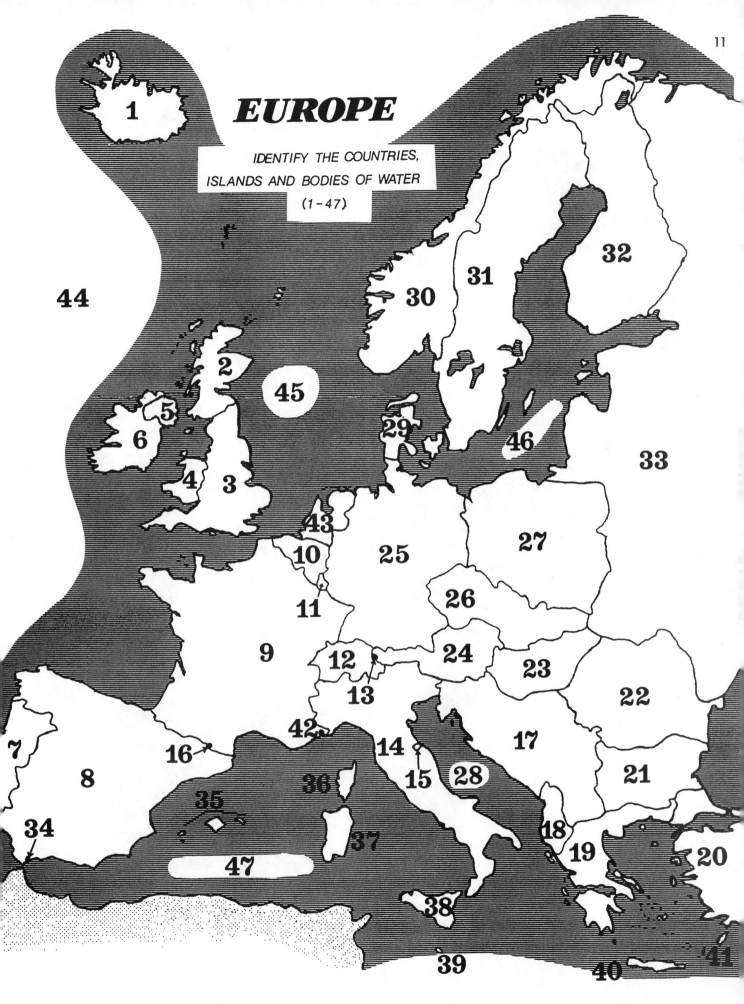

EUROPE

IDENTIFY THE COUNTRIES,
ISLANDS AND BODIES OF WATER
(1-47)

12

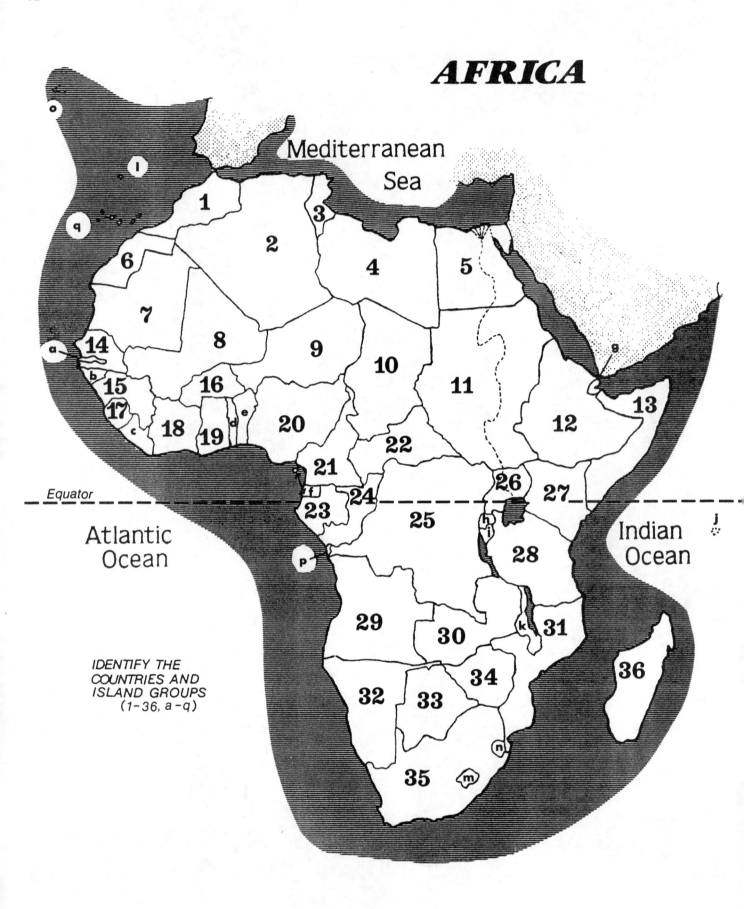

AFRICA

Mediterranean
Sea

1

3

2

4

5

6

7

8

9

10

11

12

13

14

15

16

17

18

19

20

21

22

23

24

25

26

27

28

29

30

31

32

33

34

35

36

Equator

Atlantic
Ocean

Indian
Ocean

IDENTIFY THE
COUNTRIES AND
ISLAND GROUPS
(1-36, a-q)

13

IDENTIFY
THESE COUNTRIES
(1–41)

SEA OF
OKHOTSK

Pacific
Ocean

SOUTH
CHINA SEA

BAY OF
BENGAL

ARABIAN
SEA

ARAL
SEA

CASPIAN
SEA

BLACK
SEA

RED SEA

The
Middle East
and Asia

1
2
3
4
5
6
7
8
9
10
11
12
13
14
15
16
17
18
19
20
21
22
23
24
25
26
27
28
29
30
31
32
33
34
35
36
37
39
40
41

14

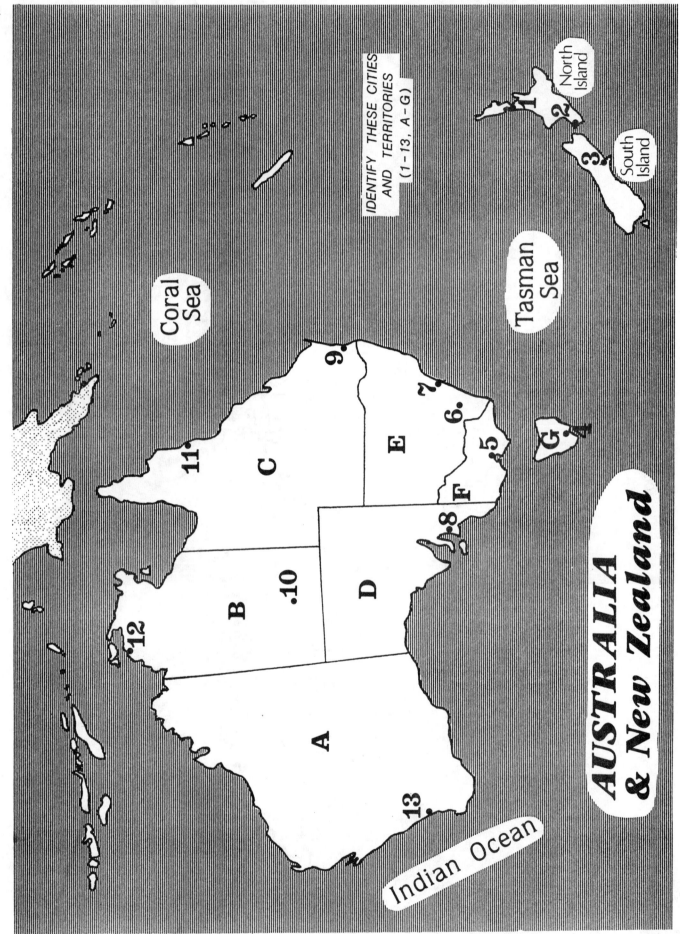

North
Island

South
Island

IDENTIFY THESE CITIES
AND TERRITORIES
(1-13, A-G)

Coral
Sea

Tasman
Sea

9.

7.

6.

E

5

G

11.

C

F

.8

D

.10

B

A

12

13.

AUSTRALIA
& New Zealand

Indian Ocean

GEOGRAPHY PROFICIENCY

MATCH THE FOLLOWING CAPITALS TO U.S. STATES:

1. ____Jefferson City   A. Illinois
2. ____Sacramento   B. Kentucky
3. ____Carson City   C. South Dakota
4. ____Springfield   D. Virginia
5. ____Pierre   E. Missouri
6. ____Salem   F. Wyoming
7. ____Richmond   G. Oregon
8. ____Madison   H. California
9. ____Cheyenne   I. Wisconsin
10. ____Frankfort   J. Nevada

MATCH THE FOLLOWING CAPITALS TO CENTRAL AMERICAN COUNTRIES:

11. ____Tegucigalpa   K. Honduras
12. ____Belmopan   L. Nicaragua
13. ____Managua   M. Costa Rica
14. ____San Jose   N. Belize

MATCH THE FOLLOWING CITIES TO CARIBBEAN ISLANDS:

15. ____Nassau   O. St. Thomas
16. ____Fort-de-France   P. St. Maarten
17. ____Santo Domingo   Q. Jamaica
18. ____Kingston   R. New Providence Is.
19. ____San Juan   S. St. Croix
20. ____Georgetown   T. Grand Cayman
21. ____Philipsburg   U. St. Martin
22. ____Marigot   V. Puerto Rico
23. ____Orangestad   W. Martinique
24. ____Charlotte Amalie   X. Aruba
25. ____Christiansted   Y. Dominican Republic

MATCH THE FOLLOWING CAPITALS TO SOUTH AMERICAN COUNTRIES:

26. _____ Bogota   A. Suriname

27. _____ Buenos Aires   B. Chile

28. _____ Quito   C. Colombia

29. _____ Santiago   D. Ecuador

30. _____ Paramaribo   E. Argentina

MATCH THE FOLLOWING CAPITALS TO EUROPEAN COUNTRIES:

31. _____ Bucharest   F. Poland

32. _____ Copenhagen   G. Finland

33. _____ Oslo   H. Greece

34. _____ Warsaw   I. Romania

35. _____ Budapest   J. Belgium

36. _____ Prague   K. Norway

37. _____ Vienna   L. Denmark

38. _____ Helsinki   M. Austria

39. _____ Athens   N. Czechoslovakia

40. _____ Brussels   O. Hungary

MATCH THE FOLLOWING CAPITALS TO AFRICAN COUNTRIES:

41. _____ Abidjan   P. Egypt

42. _____ Cairo   Q. Kenya

43. _____ Kinshasa   R. Zimbabwe

44. _____ Dar es Salaam   S. Senegal

45. _____ Harare   T. Cote d'Ivoire

46. _____ Tripoli   U. Zaire

47. _____ Monrovia   V. Tanzania

48. _____ Accra   W. Ghana

49. _____ Nairobi   X. Liberia

50. _____ Dakar   Y. Libya

MATCH THE FOLLOWING CAPITALS TO MIDDLE EAST AND ASIA COUNTRIES:

1. ____Tehran
2. ____Damascus
3. ____Beirut
4. ____Tokyo
5. ____Jakarta
6. ____Dacca
7. ____Kabul
8. ____Kathmandu
9. ____Islamabad
10. ____Port Moresby

A. Indonesia
B. Japan
C. Nepal
D. Syria
E. Pakistan
F. Lebanon
G. Bangladesh
H. Iran
I. Afghanistan
J. Papua New Guinea

MATCH THE FOLLOWING CITIES TO COUNTRIES/PACIFIC ISLANDS:

11. ____Wellington
12. ____Perth
13. ____Papeete
14. ____Hobart
15. ____Agana
16. ____Christchurch
17. ____Honolulu
18. ____Noumea
19. ____Suva
20. ____Pago Pago
21. ____Taipei
22. ____Nuku'alofa
23. ____Vila
24. ____Kahului
25. ____Apia

K. New Zealand (N. Island)
L. Tasmania
M. New Zealand (S. Island)
N. Tahiti
O. Australia
P. Guam
Q. Tonga
R. Viti Levu (Fiji Is.)
S. New Caledonia
T. American Samoa
U. U.S. - Oahu, Hawaii
V. Taiwan
W. Western Samoa
X. U.S. - Maui, Hawaii
Y. Vanuatu

NAME THREE PLACES OF INTEREST IN EACH OF THE FOLLOWING CITIES:

1. NEW YORK _____

   _____

2. LONDON _____

   _____

3. PARIS _____

   _____

4. ROME _____

   _____

5. LOS ANGELES _____

   _____

6. BEIJING _____

   _____

7. TOKYO _____

   _____

8. NEW ORLEANS _____

   _____

9. SAN FRANCISCO _____

   _____

10. MEXICO CITY _____

    _____

11. RIO DE JANEIRO _____

    _____

12. SYDNEY _____

    _____

13. MADRID _____

    _____

14. MOSCOW _____

    _____

15. ATHENS _____

    _____

DOMESTIC TRAVEL TEST

Define the following terms:

1. through fare_____

2. open segment_____

3. direct flight_____

4. extra section_____

5. open jaw trip_____

6. class of service_____

7. booking code_____

8. stopover_____

9. interline connection_____

10. layover_____

Give the city/airport codes for the following:

11. New Orleans, LA_____   16. Nashville, TN_____

12. New York/La Guardia_____   17. Seattle, WA_____

13. Dallas/Ft. Worth_____   18. Boston, MA_____

14. Los Angeles/Int'l_____   19. Denver, CO_____

15. Washington, DC/Dulles_____ 20. Cincinnati, OH_____

Decode the following time zone codes:

21. EST_____

22. PDT_____

23. CST_____

24. MDT_____

Decode the following meal codes:

25. B_____   L_____   D_____

HOTELS, CAR RENTALS, PACKAGES AND TOURS TEST

Decode the following meal plan codes and state what is included:

1. EP_____

2. CP_____

3. MAP_____

4. BP_____

5. AP_____

Explain the following room types:

6. Single_____

7. Double_____

8. Twin_____

9. Quad_____

10. Triple_____

Answer the following questions or complete the statements given:

11. What are hotel representatives?_____

_____

12. When meals on a tour are specified as "table d'hote" it means

_____

13. If the meals provided on a tour are "a la carte" it means

_____

14. Name five major car rental companies._____

_____

15. Name three reference books for hotel information._____

_____

16. Most hotels (other than resort areas) will hold a room until _____ p.m. without a guarantee.

17. Name six major hotel chains._____

_____

18. What is the difference between a standard class hotel and a first

class hotel?_____

19. If your client does not have a major credit card, are there any

other ways available for renting a car? (provided he/she meets

the sufficient age requirement)_____

_____

20. What is the difference between a package and a tour?_____

_____

21. Name four advantages of taking a tour._____

_____

22. Name three disadvantages of taking a tour._____

_____

23. Name six tour companies._____

_____

24. Name five items/components that are normally provided on a tour.

_____

25. What is the difference between a tour company and a travel agency?

_____

_____

_____

INTERNATIONAL TRAVEL REVIEW

1. What is needed to obtain a U. S. passport?_____

   _____

2. What is a visa?_____

   _____

3. What types of insurance are normally made available to clients
   through a full service travel agency?_____

   _____

Give currency names and ISO codes for the following countries:

4. Hong Kong_____

5. Colombia_____

6. Bahamas_____

7. Australia_____

8. Japan_____

9. India_____

10. Mexico_____

Give city/airport codes for the following cities:

11. Cairo, Egypt_____   16. Manila, Philippines_____

12. London, U.K./Heathrow_____ 17. Tokyo, Japan/Narita_____

13. Paris, France/Orly_____   18. Papeete, Tahiti_____

14. Brussels, Belgium_____   19. Moscow, U.S.S.R._____

15. Copenhagen, Denmark_____ 20. Acapulco, Mexico_____

Decode the following airline codes:

21. SR_____ 24. KX_____

22. JL_____ 25. TW_____

23. BA_____

TEST ON CRUISES

Match the following ships with their cruise lines:

1. _____NORWAY   A. NORWEGIAN CRUISE LINE

2. _____SONG OF AMERICA   B. CARNIVAL CRUISE LINE

3. _____CELEBRATION   C. PRINCESS CRUISES

4. _____SUN PRINCESS   D. CUNARD LINE

5. _____QUEEN ELIZABETH II   E. ROYAL CARIBBEAN CRUISE LINE

Answer the following questions:

6. What are stabilizers?_____

_____

7. What does embarkation mean?_____

8. What is the gangway?_____

9. Give four advantages of a cruise vacation._____

_____

10. Name three disadvantages of a cruise._____

_____

11. Name three staff members on a cruise who normally receive tips.

_____

12. Name three responsibilities of the purser and his/her staff.

_____

13. The left side of the ship is the _____side.

14. The right side of the ship is the _____side.

15. A ship's size is measured in _____.

16. Name five areas of the world for cruises._____

_____

Decode the following ship prefixes:

17. S/S_____   19. M/V_____

18. T/S_____   20. M/S_____

TRAVEL AGENCY PROFICIENCY TEST

Decode these airline codes:

1. AZ_____   4. SA_____

2. SN_____   5. CX_____

3. TP_____   6. TG_____

Encode these airlines:

7. Air Canada_____   9. Singapore Airlines_____

8. Air New Zealand_____   10. Philippine Airlines_____

Decode these fare bases, using your knowledge of fare indicators:

11. YG10_____

12. BE140_____

13. HXE56_____

14. VLE6M_____

15. F_____

16. C_____

17. MOE78_____

18. BHE165_____

19. YLAP60_____

20. YGV15_____

Match the following currencies with the appropriate country:

21. _____Peso   A. Mexico

22. _____Dollar   B. India

23. _____Lira   C. Turkey

24. _____Shekel   D. Israel

25. _____Rupee   E. Australia

TRAVEL AGENCY PROFICIENCY TEST

1. ARUNK is used for _____ .

2. Name five resort cities in Mexico. _____

    _____

3. What is the difference between an outside and an inside cabin

    on a cruise? _____

4. A room to be occupied by one person is a _____ room.

5. A room to be occupied by three people is a _____ room.

6. What can be the difference between a standard and a superior

    room? _____

7. How long are U.S. passports valid, if you are over 18? _____

8. What does CLIA stand for? _____

    _____

9. Name three types of insurance that clients may need in conjunc-

    tion with their travel arrangements. _____

    _____

10. What is the difference between an escorted and a hosted tour?

    _____

11. What does FIT stand for? _____

12. What is the FAA and what are its responsibilities? _____

    _____

13. What are hotel representatives? _____

    _____

14. What is the minimum age generally required for a child to travel

    unaccompanied on U.S. airlines using direct flights? _____

15. Name six popular destination islands in the Caribbean. _____

    _____

TRAVEL AGENCY PROFICIENCY TEST

Name four cities in each of the following countries:

1. France_____

2. Italy_____

3. Australia_____

4. Japan_____

5. Brazil_____

6. Canada_____

7. England_____

8. Spain_____

9. Germany_____

10. U.S.S.R._____

Decode the following city/airport codes: (name city and country)

11. NAS_____

12. NBO_____

13. LHR_____

14. YYZ_____

15. CLT_____

16. FCO_____

17. STT_____

18. NRT_____

19. ORD_____

20. MCO_____

21. CCS_____

22. ITO_____

23. PPT_____

24. SYD_____

25. SEA_____

TRAVEL AGENCY PROFICIENCY TEST

1. Name the countries of Central America._____

    _____

2. The Queen Elizabeth II is about 25,000 tons. True or False_____

3. Copenhagen is the capital of _____.

4. The area called the "Outback" is in the country of _____.

5. The meal plan code MAP means that breakfast, lunch and dinner are

    included daily. True or False_____

6. Name ten capital cities in Europe._____

    _____

7. Name ten tour companies._____

    _____

8. Name five cruise lines._____

    _____

9. Name three travel industry magazines or travel news publications.

    _____

10. Name the four major time zones of the U.S. from west to east.

    _____

11. What does the frequency code X67 mean?_____

12. Name five major hotel chains._____

    _____

13. Define the term "direct flight."_____

    _____

14. What does "run of the house" rate mean?_____

    _____

15. Name three ships that are operated by Carnival Cruise Line._____

    _____

PRODUCT KNOWLEDGE AND USE OF REFERENCES TEST

Note: Information may change after printing and answers may vary.

1. Name three companies that have tours to Scandinavia.

    _____

2. Name three cruise ships sailing from Miami that have 7 night
    cruises to the Caribbean._____

3. Name a company that specializes in tours for singles.

    _____

4. What are five areas/destinations for clients interested in scuba
    diving?_____

5. Name three car rental companies that have locations in many major
    cities in Europe._____

6. What two tour companies can you name that offer deluxe tours of
    the Orient?_____

7. For clients wanting a ski vacation in Colorado, what five ski
    resort areas can you name?_____

8. How much is baggage insurance for a client who wants $1,000 worth
    of coverage for a 14 day itinerary?_____

9. Name two cars in the compact class category offered by Hertz Car
    Rental company._____

10. Give the approximate hotel rates for a single room at the Waldorf
    Astoria Hotel in New York City._____

11. Your client wants to take a train from Paris to Zurich. Is there
    a Euro-City (Trans-European Express) train available?_____
    Give a possible train schedule (express or other). _____

    _____

    How much would a first class ticket cost?_____

12. If your client wanted to charter a yacht around the U.S. Virgin Islands, how would you obtain information?_____

_____

13. What number do you call to make reservations at a Hyatt Hotel if you are a travel agent in Chicago, IL?_____

14. Name two companies that offer deluxe tours of South America.

_____

15. If your client wanted to take an Amtrak train from New York to Chicago, what schedules and prices could you provide?_____

_____

_____

16. Name two deluxe hotels located in the French Quarter area of New Orleans, LA._____

17. How can you find out what city provides the nearest air service for Pewaukee, WI?_____

_____

What is the city?_____

18. What resources can you use to determine if the electric current in the Dominican Republic can accommodate U.S. hair dryer plugs?

_____

Does your client need an adapter?_____

19. What is the approximate temperature range in Rome, Italy, during the month of December?_____What sources can you use to obtain this information?_____

20. How can you find out the cost of a second class train ticket from Munich to Frankfurt?_____

What is the approximate cost?_____

21. If your client wanted to know how much it would cost to park at New York's La Guardia airport for 3 days, how could you find out?

_____

22. Name two sources that can be used to obtain a description of a particular hotel._____

23. Your client asks you what is the nationality of the crew on the cruise ship Fantasy of Carnival Cruise Lines. What resources can you check and what is the answer?_____

_____

24. How many hours time difference is there between New York and Rome, Italy?_____Name three resources containing that information.

_____

25. What is the tonnage of the ship called the Song of America? _____Name three ways to determine this information._____

_____

26. If your client is a Canadian citizen going to the Bahamas, how can you obtain information on the documentary requirements?_____

_____

What is required for a Canadian citizen to travel to the Bahamas?

_____

27. What references can you check for information on the ferry service schedules from Haines, Alaska to Sitka, Alaska?_____

_____

28. If a client asks about an archaeology tour to Peru, what sources would you consult to obtain some tour company names?_____

_____

29. Give the toll-free number for Qantas Airlines if you are in New York._____

30. Approximately how long does it take to fly from Los Angeles to Stockholm?_____Where can you find this information?

_____

31. What river flows through Austin, TX?_____What sources provide that fact?_____

32. If a client wants information about charter flights to Rio de Janeiro from Miami, how can you find out?_____

_____

33. If you needed to write the consulate office of Brazil, where could you obtain the address?_____

_____

34. Do they celebrate Labor Day in Czechoslovakia?_____What sources have the information?_____

_____

35. What areas for sightseeing are available from Phoenix, AZ other than the Grand Canyon?_____

_____

Name five resources that can be used to obtain this information?

_____

36. Name three ways to find out what the currency of India is and the present exchange rate._____

37. Which airlines have ticket counters/offices in Paducah, KY?_____
_____What references have this infor-
mation?_____

38. Is the Hertz car rental counter in Boston airport open 24 hours? _____How can you find out?_____

39. What resources will tell you how much photographic equipment a client can bring into Poland?_____

32

40. If clients want to go on a cruise offering activities for their two children ages 8 and 9, how can you find out what cruise ships to suggest?_____

_____

41. What sources will give you the names of dude ranches in Colorado?

_____

42. How can you find out for your client what times the banks are normally open in Brussels, Belgium?_____

_____

43. What sources can be used to find a hotel very near the Eiffel Tower in Paris, France?_____

44. If clients wanted to take a ballooning tour in France, how can you obtain some information?_____

_____

45. Where can you find out what ferry services are available from southern England to Belgium that can accommodate both passengers and cars?_____

_____

46. Approximately how long does it take by train to travel from London, England to Glasgow, Scotland?_____Name three ways to obtain that information._____

_____

47. Where can you find information on the opening and closing hours of Opryland in Nashville, TN during the month of August?_____

_____

48. How can you obtain information on renting a camper/van in New Zealand for about two weeks?_____

_____

REFERENCES AND RESOURCES REVIEW

WHERE CAN YOU FIND???

For each of the items listed below, give the reference books or resources that you can use to obtain the information. List as many sources as possible.

1. DOCUMENTARY REQUIREMENTS _____

_____

2. DEPARTURE TAX FROM JAMAICA _____

_____

3. CITY NEAREST FOR AIR SERVICE FOR TRAVELING TO EMORY UNIVERSITY _____

_____

4. CRUISES ON THE NILE - ALL DETAILS _____

_____

5. BIRD WATCHING TOUR IN COSTA RICA _____

_____

6. FREIGHTER TRIP TO AFRICA _____

_____

7. PENSIONS IN BARCELONA, SPAIN _____

_____

8. NUMBER OF ROLLS OF FILM ALLOWED TO BRING INTO CZECHOSLOVAKIA _____

_____

9. ELECTRIC CURRENT USED IN HAITI _____

_____

10. RAIL SCHEDULE FOR THE BULLET TRAIN IN JAPAN _____

_____

11. BUDGET RENT A CAR'S LOCATIONS IN LOS ANGELES _____

_____

12. DETAILS ON THE HANDICAPPED FACILITIES AT DALLAS/FT.WORTH AIRPORT ____

_____

13. COST OF PARKING AT NEW YORK/JFK AIRPORT _____

_____

14. WHEN THE RUNNING OF THE BULLS IN PAMPLOMA, SPAIN TAKES PLACE _____

_____

34

15. NEAREST CITY FOR AIR SERVICE FOR NANTES, FRANCE _____

_____

16. IF THE HYATT REGENCY AT CHICAGO O'HARE AIRPORT HAS AN INDOOR POOL ___

_____

17. DISTANCE IN MILES FROM FRANKFURT TO MUNICH _____

_____

18. PRICE OF A FIRST CLASS TRAIN TICKET FROM PARIS TO ZURICH _____

_____

19. BALLOONING TOURS IN FRANCE _____

_____

20. TRAIN SCHEDULES FROM MIAMI TO NEW YORK CITY _____

_____

21. IF A CLIENT CAN BRING BACK PINEAPPLES FROM HAWAII _____

_____

22. EXCHANGE RATE FOR U.S. DOLLARS TO DRACHMAS _____

_____

23. WHAT DATES MARDI GRAS TAKES PLACE IN NEW ORLEANS _____

_____

24. HOW MUCH IS A 15 DAY EURAILPASS _____

_____

25. WHAT SHOTS/INOCULATIONS ARE NECESSARY TO TRAVEL FROM U.S. TO ZAIRE __

_____

26. CASTLE ACCOMMODATIONS IN ENGLAND _____

_____

27. IF IT IS SAFE TO TRAVEL TO GUATEMALA _____

_____

28. WEATHER TO EXPECT IN ROME IN JANUARY _____

_____

29. HOTELS NEAR THE INTERNATIONAL AIRPORT IN MIAMI _____

_____

30. IF THE HERTZ CAR RENTAL DESK IS OPEN 24 HOURS AT JFK AIRPORT _____

_____

SALES TECHNIQUES

A travel agent or travel counselor is also a salesperson. As with any other sales position, there are certain techniques and procedures that will lead to profitable selling. "Making the sale" is something that is beneficial to you, your client, and the agency in which you work. Sometimes the word "salesperson" or "selling" can bring images of high pressure sales and unethical practices to mind. It is selling without these tactics that is most productive in the travel industry, and this is the aspect of selling that will be considered here.

Selling in a successful manner does not always come naturally. You can be the most knowledgeable person in the agency, but the worst salesperson. There are basic principles of selling and a psychology to selling. Implementation of these principles and the psychology behind them can vary, depending on your personality, the area of the country, the type of clientele, and other factors.

First, let us cover the outline of successful selling. The travel agent has to:

* OBTAIN ALL THE NECESSARY INFORMATION (WHO, WHEN, WHERE, HOW MANY)

* QUALIFY THE CLIENT AND DETERMINE THE CLIENT'S NEEDS AND BUDGET

* MAKE SUGGESTIONS, ASK MORE QUESTIONS, HELP ANALYZE OPTIONS

* RESERVE SPACE, HANDLE OBJECTIONS, SUGGEST UPGRADES OR CHANGES

* OBTAIN THE CLIENT'S COMMITMENT AND CLOSE THE SALE

* WORK THROUGH TO THE CLIENT'S DEPARTURE

* FOLLOW UP AND CONTACT THE CLIENT SOME WEEKS AFTER THE TRIP

Now, let us look more "in depth" at a "sale situation" - with specific procedures and professional techniques.

AN IN-DEPTH LOOK AT THE SALES SITUATION

Certain bookings for a client may be simple "order-taking" situations; others may involve lengthy processes. Let's take a closer look at the details of advising and selling travel products and an elaboration of professional techniques:

1. **GREET THE CLIENT AND INTRODUCE YOURSELF.** If the client is on the phone, follow the **RULES OF TELEPHONE COURTESY** on page 53. If the client is in your office, greet them and introduce yourself. Stand up, smile, and say "Good morning (or "good afternoon" or "hello"), I'm Maryann Burns." Use eye-to-eye-contact and shake hands as you guide the client to a seat. As you have given your name, the client will most likely state his name. Try to use the client's name at least twice in the course of the conversation. If all the agents are busy when a client enters the office, someone should at least "recognize" the client by smiling at them and letting them know that someone will be with them as soon as possible. These initial contacts are crucial elements of making a sale and they lead to long-term profitability.

2. **OBTAIN THE NECESSARY INFORMATION:**

   WHO and HOW MANY - names, addresses, phone numbers, ages

   WHERE - destination, possible destinations, interests

   WHEN - dates, possible dates, alternative dates

   AT WHAT COST - what type of budget, preference of accommodations (If client avoids stating an amount, give several ranges to choose from; i.e., "Would you like to spend under $300.00 per person, under $500.00 per person, under $1000.00 per person, under $2000.00, under $3000.00," etc.)

   ASK CITIZENSHIP AND GO OVER DOCUMENTS AND SHOTS NECESSARY, if an international trip is involved.

   YOU MAY WANT TO ASK WHAT INFORMATION/FARES HAVE ALREADY BEEN OBTAINED. This will be helpful if the client has "shopped around" and is simply searching for "the cheapest fare." It avoids duplication of work done by other agents. You can also point out that price is just one item and there are other factors (convenience, preference of accommodations, the client's likes and dislikes, and trip expectations) to consider.

3. **QUALIFY THE CLIENT.** If time permits, use the **TRAVELER'S PROFILE FORM** provided on the next page. This will serve as a profile and record of your client to which you can refer and update as necessary. You may have the client complete it beforehand or go over the questions at your desk.

```
TRAVELER'S PROFILE FORM                    Date:_____

Name_____ Home Phone_____

Address_____ Work Phone_____

City/State/Zip_____Birthdate(optional)_____

Citizenship_____ Do you have a valid passport?_____

Your profession or business?_____About how many trips
do you take a year?_____ How many are out of the country?_____ About what
percent are business trips?_____   What percent are for pleasure?_____

Which areas have you visited?____Florida ____Calif. ____Hawaii ____Alaska
____Mexico ____Canada ____Caribbean ____Cntrl.Amer. ____South America
____Europe ____Africa ____Middle East ____Asia ____Australia/S.Pacific

Name areas that you are interested in traveling to_____

_____

Do you prefer to travel independently or with a group?_____

Do you prefer deluxe, first class or standard accommodations?_____

What do you usually enjoy doing on your vacation? (check any that apply)
____guided tours  ____gourmet dining  ____good beaches  ____sightseeing
____shopping  ____nightlife  ____relaxing  ____meeting people  ____events
sports(__golf __tennis __diving __hiking __camping  other_____)

What tour companies have you used before?_____

_____ Any comments on them?_____

_____ Have you ever taken a cruise?_____

Would you like to?_____ If you have cruise experience, what ships and areas?

Do you prefer any ships/cruise lines?_____

_____

What is the most you would normally spend per person on your vacation?

__under $1000  __$1000-2000  __$2000-3000  __$3000-4000  __over $4000

Do you have any medical conditions/allergies that should be considered?____

_____
Are there any frequent flyer/traveler programs you would like considered?

_____

Club/organization memberships:_____
```

4. **MAKE SUGGESTIONS OF DESTINATIONS, COMPANIES, ETC., OR GO OVER THE BROCHURES** the client has perhaps already chosen. This is the "answering questions"/"analyzing options" stage. Factors such as weather, events, interests, travel experiences and expectations enter into the recommendations. The agent "guides" the client through this decision-making process, always providing information and advice in such a way that the client really makes the decisions. For example, clients may want to rely on your choice of hotel. Rather than picking a hotel for your client, describe three/four properties and then the client is better equipped to decide on one.

5. **RESERVE SPACE.** If the client starts to balk or seems unsure or objecting, **GIVE MORE INFORMATION.** A good way to "flow through" this stage is to agree with the client and then evaluate the circumstance or objection to find a solution. For example, the client suddenly states: "You know, I really don't think I can afford this trip." You can offer the following suggestions:

> I have some information on a less expensive cruise/hotel - here is one that averages at least $100.00 less.

OR

> If we move the dates to two months later, you could start a savings plan of putting something like $100.00 a month into an account so that the trip is affordable. What about the dates of Sept. 15 to 20 instead of July?

OR

> If you have a major credit card, you can charge the $200.00 deposit to hold the reservation.

There are many ways to overcome objections, and in some cases a more detailed look at the client's likes and dislikes will warrant the consideration of an UPGRADE. Maybe the client saw a flyer offering an inexpensive package but really would like a more deluxe tour. Provide more information to make appropriate decisions.

6. **COVER THE DETAILS OF PAYMENTS REQUIRED, DEADLINES, PROCESSING OF DOCUMENTS, TICKETING, ETC.** If possible, collect the deposit from the client; write down for the client and indicate on your calendar or computer the other deadlines for payments. Provide/suggest reading materials and activities that would be of benefit for the client's trip.

7. **SMILE AND THANK THE CLIENT,** and perhaps stand up and shake hands as the client is leaving. If the client has telephoned, thank him and project a "smile" in your voice.

8. **MAINTAIN THE SCHEDULE AND COMMUNICATION WITH THE CLIENT CONCERNING DETAILS THAT COME UP REGARDING THE ITINERARY.** Go over documents, tickets and other vouchers before handing/sending them to the client - check for errors, omissions, changes. Explain any last minute items, reconfirmation, hotel taxes, departure taxes, etc.

9. **MAKE A CALL A FEW WEEKS AFTER THE CLIENT'S RETURN AND ASK FOR ANY COMMENTS THAT WOULD BE HELPFUL TO OTHER CLIENTS, OR MAIL THE CLIENT A "WELCOME BACK" POSTCARD.**

10. **KEEP IN TOUCH WITH SPECIAL OFFERS OR NEW TRIP PRODUCTS THAT YOU THINK YOUR CLIENT WOULD LIKE. REVIEW THE CLIENT'S FILE FOR PLANNING ANNUAL TRIPS, ETC. IF POSSIBLE, DO MAILINGS TO A CUSTOMER BASE ON TRAVEL NEWS AND SPECIALS.**

SOME OTHER MAJOR POINTS TO CONSIDER

Deciding on <u>when</u> to close the sale depends on the client and the situation.

Always ask OPEN-ENDED questions, not CLOSE-ENDED questions. Ask questions that <u>cannot</u> be answered by "Yes" or "No." For example: Would the 15th or 21st be better?
<u>Not</u>: Shall I try to reserve the 15th?

Sell the **benefits** not the features. The benefit is something personalized for the client. Cruises are all-inclusive, but for your client the benefit is that no major expenses are incurred once they are on board (just tipping, alcoholic beverages, shore excursions, and souvenir purchases).

Use your own or third party experiences to help assure the client. EXAMPLE: "I've had several clients who really enjoyed this Panama Canal cruise."

Don't talk too much or oversell. Be realistic. Point out any important items. EXAMPLE: "When in Mexico it is best to drink bottled water and drinks without ice. Also, peel fruits and eat only cooked vegetables since different pesticides are used in some countries."

Be sincere. Project enthusiasm. If you don't know the answer to a question, explain that you will be happy to find out.

40

* *

Remember to provide the client with COMPLETE TRAVEL SERVICES.

THE TRIP INCLUDES:

* possible travel documentation requirements

* transportation to and from the destination

* accommodations

* other transportation needs

* possible sightseeing tours

* meals and tipping

* taxes, travel insurance and other details

SUCCESSFUL SALES TECHNIQUES

To be successful and professional in the travel industry requires

SELF-KNOWLEDGE

CLIENT KNOWLEDGE AND INDUSTRY AWARENESS

PRODUCT KNOWLEDGE

PRESENTATION KNOWLEDGE

* *

SELF-KNOWLEDGE

Improve your self-knowledge by evaluating yourself, your personality and attitude. This involves a process of knowing your good qualities and working on any weaknesses that may inhibit your job performance. One of the most important attributes is to

HAVE A POSITIVE MENTAL ATTITUDE

A glass filled halfway with water is HALF-FULL, not HALF-EMPTY. "You can never succeed unless you try." "What you conceive, you can work to achieve." "If at first you don't succeed, try, try again." These are examples of positive thinking.

If you tend to be a "moaner" and a "groaner" about going to work, job duties, the actions of your fellow employees or your boss, or just about anything, then it's time to REEVALUATE. Start to work at thinking POSITIVELY about your situation. Look on the bright side of things. If you hate your job, find out what EXACTLY will help you like it (changing positions in the company, switching to another location, discussing with your boss your need for a salary increase, a vacation, whatever). Take an evaluative look at yourself as if you were another person. Would you be happy to work with you? Do you make things pleasant for the clients and people around you? Are you motivated, enthusiastic, helpful and eager to do things?

Do you have a POSITIVE MENTAL ATTITUDE?

Half-full or half-empty?

Another necessary quality of a travel professional is to

BE ORGANIZED AND ACCURATE

Be on time or even early to work, do things without being told, make certain all your work is accurate. Organize your desk and resources so that you can work effectively. Make lists of things to do and label them A, B, or C according to their priority.

No matter how organized and accurate you are, you are human and there may be a time you have made a mistake. If so, admit it and apologize. Try to provide some type of compensation if possible. The error can only be compounded by not admitting fault if the client finds out later who was really to blame.

THINGS TO DO

A. Mr. Smith's cruise and tour.
B. Itinerary planning for the
   Rodriquez family this summer.
C. Read trade magazines for
   upcoming seminars.

ME?
MAKE A MISTAKE?
I SURE DID!!!!

I'm so sorry!

* *

A vital need for working in a sales and service industry such as travel is to

HAVE GOOD COMMUNICATION SKILLS

This means the ability to EXPLAIN and DISCUSS details, as well as to LISTEN effectively. Communicate in an organized manner. Think before you speak. And you can only LISTEN if you have STOPPED TALKING.

The next pages provide a list for practicing effective listening skills.

LISTENING SKILLS

1. **LOOK AT THE OTHER PERSON.** Eye to eye contact is most important for communication to be effective. It will help ensure your concentration as well as your client's, and it indicates to the client that he is important and has your attention.

2. **GET RID OF DISTRACTIONS.** This isn't easy, as busy as you are sometimes. Avoid taking phone calls. If possible, have messages taken. If you must take a call, make it brief, giving preference to the client who has taken the time to come to your office. Do not continue doing paperwork while talking to the client; you may make a serious error trying to do two things at once.

3. **CONTROL BUT DON'T DOMINATE THE CONVERSATION.** Lead the client in the conversation. If a client starts to digress from necessary information, gently guide the conversation back to pertinent areas without being rude or inconsiderate.

4. **ASK QUESTIONS AND EXPLAIN ANSWERS.** If a client has mentioned a place or name with which you are not familiar, ask questions regarding the matter. Do not assume or ignore anything as it may be important. Do not use industry jargon to explain things. Speak in a manner the client can understand. Also, do not "talk down" to the client, intone sarcasm or embarrass the client.

5. **THINK ABOUT WHAT THE CLIENT IS SAYING.** Be aware of the client's tone of voice and what he is saying. Observe the non-verbal communication: the client's "body language" may be communicating fear, anger, etc.

6. **ORGANIZE BY CATEGORIZING AND OUTLINING**. Give information in a detailed and organized way. Don't start talking about the cancellation penalties and then switch to talking about best buys. Determine what the client likes and dislikes by giving categories of information. Outline the trip details in an organized and logical way. For example:

> In planning your trip, Mr. Kirkonnel, we need to first look at the flights to Hawaii, then the transportation to your choice of hotel, the accommodations you desire, and any sightseeing or special events that you would like arranged.

7. **TAKE NOTES**. Write down important dates, places, names. Take notes of what the client is saying so he doesn't have to repeat information.

8. **REMEMBER THE DIFFERENCE IN SPEAKING AS OPPOSED TO LISTENING.** The average thinking/listening rate is about 500 words a minute, while the normal speaking rate is 100-150 words a minute. Keep the client interested by showing him the brochure while explaining the trip details and amenities. However, this does not mean that you should race through the information or make the client feel rushed.

9. **MAKE THE CLIENT FEEL THAT HE IS MAKING THE DECISIONS**. Give choices and perhaps recommendations or suggestions, but make the client feel that he has made the decisions. In this way, if the client was disappointed in the destination or accommodations, he will feel in part responsible.

10. **BE A GOOD LISTENER**. Remember that you have to STOP TALKING to LISTEN. Use the points given, be alert, sit up straight, and project enthusiasm and understanding. You will be successful in acquiring and keeping clients!

CLIENT KNOWLEDGE AND INDUSTRY AWARENESS

Most clients use a travel agent because they feel their needs and interests will be considered and acted upon. Most successful agents have established a good relationship with their clients. They have come to know and like their clients and their clients have come to depend on the agent. The client considers the agent knowledgeable, competent, and considerate of their demands and trip requirements. The agent has acquired a "clientele" who rely on him/her every time they need travel arrangements.

The best way to "know" a client is to ask a lot of questions and to retain the answers for future consideration. The **Traveler's Profile Form** and the information that can be stored in the computer are all part of the establishment of the relationship.

Unlike the sale of other products, travel is an **experience**. You provide the details and documents, but so much of the "success" of the trip depends on the suppliers and vendors used. And yet, some clients feel that you, the agent, are ultimately responsible.

With increased competition, growth, and proliferation of franchises, travel clubs, etc. and the extent of deregulation with airlines and all other suppliers using "direct to the public" sales alternatives and marketing, travel agencies are now more than ever retailers of unregulated, volatile and variable-priced products. The hazards of discounts, rebates, and non-commissionable sales have become a familiar part of agency operations.

Travel is an ever-changing industry and today's "customer market" is composed of sophisticated, educated travelers and consumers. They have "shopped" around - as everyone does when they are about to make a major purchase. The vendors are going direct to the customer if it will help in the competitive battle to gain sales. Agencies with more volume will earn higher commissions, overrides, and be entitled to special prices.

THE SMALLER AGENCY AND INDIVIDUAL AGENTS CAN SURVIVE BY:

*providing a professional service - people are willing to pay and want to feel they are being properly informed and treated well when spending a great deal of money.

*having the information and product knowledge - which is why the client has chosen to use your services in the first place. Have the resources available to answer questions and give out that "extra helpful" information.

*developing a "niche" or specialty area in which your agency or you can excel (ski trips, honeymoons, family vacations, adventure travel, singles' tours, environmental trips, etc.).

*educating the consumer - explain why and how you can help their dreams and plans become a reality. Many agents simply "give up" on sales by not explaining/researching/communicating enough with the client.

*establishing customer loyalty by providing "personal" services such as detailed itineraries and general information (maps, handouts) and extras such as birthday cards, anniversary cards, "welcome back" postcards, "bon voyage" gifts, etc.

*promoting - by direct mail, telemarketing, public relations efforts, fundraisers, advertising, newsletters, etc.

*joining industry and other professional organizations for opportunities to network with industry leaders and obtain client and industry contacts.

*attending conferences, seminars, trade shows and industry events.

*looking to the future and planning - keep "two steps ahead" by reading everything you can get your hands on - current events, new product details, training manuals, management strategies, and information about the competition.

PRODUCT KNOWLEDGE

Product knowledge encompasses the technical skills of working on computers, ticketing procedures, fare research, accounting, documentation, travel specifics, plus many other areas such as knowledge of destinations, travel products and services, current trends, and where to find information.

How can you build product knowledge?

Start by seeing the BIG PICTURE.

Realize that you can't possibly know everything, but you DO know some things and CAN WORK on knowing more, step by step.

Employ the following helpful items for self-improvement and progress in technical and professional development:

*Start building a resource library of your own. Members of AAA (American Automobile Association) can obtain a set of tour books and maps for the U.S. and other areas for personal use. Book clubs or other travel association memberships can be useful for acquiring references and travel literature. Buy bookshelves, a filing cabinet, and collect travel sections and articles from newspapers, magazines, etc.

*Organize your drawer, desk and office to have reference notes and bulletin boards of information where they can best be used. When business is slow, read reference books, travel magazines, newspapers, and travel guides. Pick up brochures that you have never used before - to be familiar with them and to learn about itineraries used. Go through the files to throw away old brochures and simplify any filing that needs better organization.

*Learn from your fellow employees and your clients. If employees have completed a familarization trip report, pass this around so all can read the evaluations. If a certain client has sailed on 20 or more cruise ships, he can provide valuable insight into the comparison of services, facilities and ports. Most clients love to talk about what they know or have experienced on their trip and agents can use specific information to pass on to others.

*Learn from the suppliers or representatives. They are well-equipped to explain certain trip details and features, and to clarify any uncertainties about the arrangements or destinations. For example, the tour operator may know of the hotels that have rooms with king size beds.

*Read the trade press and subscribe to other travel magazines to get the consumer's point of view. Agency managers should circulate memos, important articles or magazines, have a checklist to indicate that each agent has read the information, and post advertisements and other details on a centrally located bulletin board.

*Treat familiarization trips as education and require a detailed report or briefing. Circulate the trip photographs and souvenirs to help spread the knowledge and to make it interesting.

*Hold regular staff meetings - these are a necessary vehicle for **sharing product knowledge and providing updates regarding procedures and events.**

*Attend seminars, conferences, trade shows and industry events.

*Join local, national or international associations to further your education, provide networking activities, and contacts.

*Watch local and world news, plus travel documentaries on television.

*See or rent films/videos that feature a destination or travel product.

*Read books that include details of a destination or explain an area's history, culture, etc.

*Enroll in courses at community colleges, adult centers, universities, etc.

*Learn a second or third language.

*Make trips to the library and bookstores in the area.

There are so many travel products and the industry components change so constantly. You must meet the demands of the industry and the people of the world with whom you will be in contact. You must educate and be educated. The learning will never stop, unless you impede yourself.

PRESENTATION KNOWLEDGE

After evaluating and improving your self-knowledge, client knowledge, and product knowledge, continue now to evaluating and enhancing your presentation knowledge. This is knowledge of the way you look, speak, listen, and act. The results are effective sales techniques.

THE WAY YOU LOOK

Are you neat? Do you keep your hair clean, neat, and nicely styled? Are your clothes clean, neat, and fashionable? Do you wear a modest amount of jewelry and make-up (if applicable)? Do you smile often? Do you stand and sit up straight? Does your "body language" indicate that you are interested and motivated?

THE WAY YOU SPEAK

Do you speak clearly? Do you make certain you are understood? Are you polite? Are you friendly and enthusiastic? Do you use good grammar? Do you make sure you aren't talking too loudly or too softly and that you sound pleasant and interesting? Since many travel sales are conducted over the phone, your voice is the projection of your entire image to the client. Tape your voice in a sample conversation. Maybe ask a manager or other business person to help in the evaluation. Correct problems such as using double negatives, talking too loudly or too softly, saying "yeah" instead of "yes," repeating "you know," or saying "huh" instead of "pardon me." Don't use expressions such as "You have to," "I guess," "I don't know," "It's cheaper." Say instead: "It is necessary," "I believe," "Let me find out for you," "It's less expensive." Follow the **Rules of Telephone Courtesy** on page 53.

THE WAY YOU LISTEN

Review the LISTENING SKILLS outlined previously. Write the ten "points" on an index card (or any areas that you are continually weak on) and review it periodically before communicating with clients.

THE WAY YOU ACT

Do you work until you get a job done? Do you control your temper? Do you keep promises? Is your work accurate and done quickly? Are you on time for appointments/work? Do you read things carefully? Are you organized? Do you adjust easily to problems and frustrations? Do you like people and work well with them? Do you remember things well? Are you honest and sincere? Do you make a favorable first impression? Are you agressive in a positive way? Are you unbiased and treat all people equally?

If you can't answer "yes" to the questions above, continually work on your weaknesses until you can say "yes!"

50

A PERSONAL EVALUATION

The following checklist pertains to the qualities of a successful travel professional. Be honest in indicating "yes" or "no."

COMMUNICATION SKILLS	YES	NO
1. Are you polite with people regardless of who they are?	_____	_____
2. Do you express yourself well when talking to people?	_____	_____
3. Do you listen carefully to others?	_____	_____
4. Do you make certain you are understood?	_____	_____

ATTITUDE AND PERSONAL APPEARANCE

	YES	NO
1. Do you believe you can succeed in your goals and dreams?	_____	_____
2. Are you a confident person?	_____	_____
3. Do you keep your hair clean, neat, and nicely styled?	_____	_____
4. Do you dress in a business-like manner?	_____	_____
5. If applicable, do you wear a modest amount of makeup and/or jewelry?	_____	_____
6. Do you smile frequently?	_____	_____
7. Do you work towards your goals?	_____	_____
8. Do you have a good, positive attitude?	_____	_____

WORK AND SELLING SKILLS

	YES	NO
1. Do you like to talk to people?	_____	_____
2. Do you feel comfortable with people?	_____	_____
3. Do you feel confident in talking to people?	_____	_____
4. Are you friendly to people?	_____	_____
5. Are you enthusiastic?	_____	_____
6. Do you work until you get the job done?	_____	_____
7. Do you follow rules and regulations?	_____	_____
8. Do you tell the truth?	_____	_____
9. Do you control your temper?	_____	_____
10. Do you adjust easily to problems and frustrations?	_____	_____
11. Do you work hard and accurately?	_____	_____

Copyright Claudine Dervaes

WORK AND SELLING SKILLS (continued)

12. Are you organized?   ----- -----

13. Do you keep promises?   ----- -----

14. Are you on time for work and appointments?   ----- -----

15. Do you make very few mistakes?   ----- -----

16. Do you like to read and keep up with current events?   ----- -----

17. Do you have a good memory?   ----- -----

18. Do you learn about things you don't know?   ----- -----

19. Do you always act pleasantly to people?   ----- -----

20. Do you work well with people?   ----- -----

21. Are you proud of the work you complete?   ----- -----

22. Are you aggressive in a positive way?   ----- -----

23. Do you read things carefully?   ----- -----

24. Do you understand what you read?   ----- -----

25. Do you overcome resistance?   ----- -----

26. Do you make a favorable first impression?   ----- -----

27. Are you interested in others instead of talking about
    yourself?   ----- -----

28. Are you humble about what you know and do instead of
    bragging about your skills and accomplishments?   ----- -----

29. If you have to, do you correct others in a reasonable
    and mature way?   ----- -----

30. Are you patient, considerate, and understanding?   ----- -----

---

IF THERE ARE ANY ITEMS TO WHICH YOU ANSWERED "NO,"

WORK ON THOSE CHARACTERISTICS

TO MAKE THE ANSWER "YES!"

TAKE A GOOD LOOK AT YOURSELF...

DO YOU LOOK LIKE THIS?   **OR LIKE THIS?**

DO YOU ANSWER THE PHONE LIKE THIS?   **OR LIKE THIS?**

Tape record your voice. Look in the mirror. Ask friends, relatives, business associates for advice and comments. Accept criticism as CONSTRUCTIVE AND USEFUL, and PUT POSITIVE CHANGES INTO EFFECT!

Since telephone contact with clients is so important, the development of a good telephone manner is a priority.

RULES OF TELEPHONE COURTESY

1. Answer the phone promptly and identify the company and/or yourself. You should give the impression of a courteous and efficient company the moment you answer the phone.

2. Use the caller's name and treat every call as important.

3. Be prepared to take notes. Write down the date, time, name, phone number, and message.

4. Take time to be helpful, and apologize for errors or delays. If you have to put the call on hold, WAIT for the client to respond and say "thank you for waiting" when you return to the call. If you have to transfer the call, indicate it, and make sure you transfer it to the right person.

5. Be tactful and polite. For example, say "May I say who's calling?," NOT "Who's calling?" and "Mr. Smith is out of the office right now, may I have him call you?" NOT "I don't know where he is."

6. Say "please," "thank you" and "you're welcome." Be friendly and give the call your undivided attention.

7. Avoid slang and technical terms. Cover the phone receiver if you must ask someone a question while the client is on the phone.

8. Do not chew gum, drink or eat while talking.

9. Be factual. A wrong answer is worse than none.

10. Place your own calls. It saves time and the call is more courteous.

11. When calling long distance, be sure of the phone number, and be aware of time differences.

12. Use good voice qualities: sound alert, pleasant, distinct, and expressive. Use a "voice with a smile." Talk in a normal tone and at a moderate speed.

13. End the call with your name, a warm "good-bye," or "thank you for calling," and hang up gently.

14. Return calls promptly, and be prepared with answers (if questions were given in the message).

15. If important items were discussed, make notes (with the date) in the client's file or record for future reference and documentation. Always document "what, when, and with whom" details were confirmed.

GOOD TELEPHONE TECHNIQUES

Here are some sample statements that relate professional telephone communication techniques:

Answering the phone on the first or second ring, if possible:

>   XYZ Travel, this is Nancy, how may I help you?
>
>   Good morning! ABC Tours, this is Denise.
>
>   Thank you for calling Travel Design, Mark speaking.

If you must put a call on hold:

>   Journeys and Adventures Travel, all the agents are busy
>   at this time, may I put you on hold?
>   WAIT FOR THE CLIENT TO RESPOND, and then say "thank you."

When you pick up the holding line:

>   Thank you for waiting. How may I help you?

Proceeding with the information given:

>   Yes, Mr. Fernandino, I can check for flights on the 20th
>   to Las Vegas, would you prefer a morning or afternoon
>   departure?

Providing more information to assist the client:

>   There are available seats on Friday. However, if you would
>   be able to leave on Thursday, a lower fare might be
>   available.

Giving details in a prioritized manner:

>   There is a non-stop flight that leaves Salt Lake City
>   at 9:10 am, arriving in New York/La Guardia at 4:25 pm.
>   If you need to depart later in the morning, the flights
>   have a stop or you will have to change planes.

Providing all the specifics when confirmed:

>   Your reservations are confirmed on Delta flight #345,
>   coach class, on Aug. 10, leaving Atlanta at 8:35 am,
>   arriving in Denver at 11:10 am. The return is on Delta
>   flight #678, coach class, on Aug. 19, leaving Denver
>   at 1:25 pm and arriving in Atlanta at 5:40 pm.

REVIEW ON SALES TECHNIQUES

1. Name three questions agents ask that begin with "W."

   _____   _____   _____

2. Name five factors (other than budget and preference of accommodations) that should enter into the agent's recommendations and suggestions to the client.

   a. _____

   b. _____

   c. _____

   d. _____

   e. _____

3. For successful sales techniques, the agent needs to have what four kinds of knowledge?

   a. _____

   b. _____

   c. _____

   d. _____

4. Name six items included in providing complete travel services for a client's trip.

   a. _____

   b. _____

   c. _____

   d. _____

   e. _____

   f. _____

5. What are five points of good listening skills?

   a. _____

   b. _____

   c. _____

   d. _____

   e. _____

56

6. Name seven items that can help build product knowledge.

   a. _____

   b. _____

   c. _____

   d. _____

   e. _____

   f. _____

   g. _____

7. Presentation knowledge means evaluating and improving the way you

   _____, _____, _____, _____.

8. Name six ways that the smaller agency and individual agents can
   survive in today's competitive marketplace.

   a. _____

   b. _____

   c. _____

   d. _____

   e. _____

   f. _____

9. The three key attributes mentioned under "self-knowledge" are

   a. _____

   b. _____

   c. _____

10. Good telephone techniques include: answer the phone on the _____

    or _____ ring, make sure to wait for the client to respond

    before _____, and say _____

    _____ when you pick up the holding line.

Now practice telephone and sales techniques, using the sample calls on
the next pages.

SAMPLE CALL   The agency is called Journeys to Take Travel. Using your own name, fill in the blanks with sample responses.

Phone rings, you answer _____
_____

Client: This is Harry Jones and I wanted to know how much it costs to fly to London.

You respond _____
_____

Client: I am not really sure of the dates, my wife and I were thinking of going this spring - in April or May.

You respond _____
_____
_____
_____
_____

POSSIBLE RESPONSES INCLUDE:

Journeys to Take Travel, this is _____, how may I help you?

Yes, Mr. Jones, I can research for fares to London for you - do you have specific dates of travel in mind?

The fares for travel in the spring are usually less than in the summer, which is considered peak season. In addition, if you can leave midweek instead of on the weekend it is usually less expensive. Let me look at some possible fares for travel in April, and also find out when the fares would change to the peak prices. Did you have any preference of airlines?

Client: We don't have any airline preference, but with news of some airlines filing bankruptcy, we would want a financially secure one.

You respond _____
_____
_____

Client: We have a Visa card, so that wouldn't be a problem. Can you also reserve a hotel for us in London?

You respond _____
_____

POSSIBLE RESPONSES INCLUDE:

You can use airlines that at present seem financially secure, but it's not a guarantee they will always be secure. You can purchase insurance against airline default. Paying by credit card also offers some protection.

Yes, as a full service agency we can assist with all your travel needs.

58

ANOTHER SAMPLE CALL

Phone rings, you answer _____
_____

Client: I wanted to know about cruises through the Panama Canal.

You respond _____
_____

Client: I would like to plan on October, but it depends on what it costs
and what is available. My name is Marsha Burns, and my phone
number is 888-1111.

You respond _____
_____
_____
_____

POSSIBLE RESPONSES INCLUDE:

Journeys to Take Travel, this is _____, how may I help you?

There are a few ships to choose from for Panama Canal cruises and they
are offered at different times of the year. When were you interested in
taking the cruise - and may I ask for your name and your phone number?

Thank you, Marsha. Let me get information on the ships offering Panama
Canal cruises in October. Have you taken any cruises before or do you
prefer a specific cruise line?

Client: I've been to the Bahamas and the Virgin Islands on cruises, but
I don't have any preference of cruise line. I would like a ship
that's fairly large.

You respond _____
_____
_____

Client: My cousin and I would share a cabin and we want an inexpensive
cabin so that we would to be able to enjoy the shore excursions.

You respond _____
_____

POSSIBLE RESPONSES INCLUDE:

Let me check the cruise ships that have a canal cruise in October, and
their tonnages and other details for you. Can you hold on just a moment
please? ... Thank you. Thank you for waiting, the ....and
the ....have cruises through the canal in October. The ship
that is larger is the .... Did you need a cabin for a single
and did you want a mid-priced cabin?

Yes, I can understand. Let me check what cabins are still available.

If possible, repeat the phone call exercise, with an associate acting as the client and your instructor or another person evaluating your performance and skills.

ROLE-PLAY EVALUATION

The first evaluation relates to the agent's approach and greeting:

_____USED CORRECT PHONE ANSWERING/GREETING (identified self, agency)
_____SOUNDED ENTHUSIASTIC (smile in the voice, uplifting tone)
_____SEEMED PROFESSIONAL AND PREPARED (no hesitation, organized)

Then, the agent's attitude and voice qualities:

_____SOUNDED PLEASED	_____SOUNDED NERVOUS	_____SOUNDED BORED
_____VOICE JUST RIGHT	_____VOICE TOO LOUD	_____VOICE TOO SOFT
_____GOOD RHYTHM	_____TALKED TOO FAST	_____TALKED TOO SLOWLY
_____PLEASING VOICE	_____MONOTONE	_____TOO MUCH INFLECTION

Then, the exchange of information:

_____OBTAINED WHO, WHERE, WHEN, TIME PREFERRED, RETURN DATE AND TIME
_____DETERMINED ACCEPTABLE ALTERNATIVES: NON-STOP ONLY, CONNECTIONS, ETC.
_____OBTAINED FARE CONSIDERATIONS, AIRLINE PREFERENCES, ETC.

KEY POINTS RELATING TO SPECIFIC SITUATIONS:

_____PRESENTED SPECIFIC DETAILS AND INFORMATION

_____PRESENTED BENEFITS OF FEATURES

_____USED OPEN-ENDED QUESTIONS (ones that cannot be answered with just "yes" or "no")

_____HANDLED OBJECTIONS

_____DID (OR ARRANGED TO DO) PERTINENT RESEARCH

_____OFFERED TO MAKE TENTATIVE RESERVATIONS AND THEN CONTACT THE CLIENTS TO CONFIRM THEM

_____OBTAINED RESERVATIONS

_____RECOGNIZED BUYING SIGNALS

_____COLLECTED DEPOSIT

_____ANSWERED THE CLIENTS' QUESTIONS (IF ANY)

_____MADE APPROPRIATE RECOMMENDATIONS (IF APPLICABLE)

_____CLOSED THE CALL PROFESSIONALLY/ENDED THE VISIT BY THANKING THE CLIENTS AND ASSURING THEM OF YOUR SERVICES

60

HANDLING COMPLAINTS - A SAMPLE CALL

Phone rings, you answer _____

_____

Client: This is Michelle Kravits and I need to speak to the manager.

(Manager has asked you to take all calls for the next hour)
You respond _____

Client: I don't think you can help me. I've already had enough problems
         with the agent who handled my trip plans.

You respond _____

_____

_____

POSSIBLE RESPONSES INCLUDE:

Journeys to Take Travel, this is _____, how may I help you?

The manager is not available right now, may I assist you?

I'm sorry that you are disappointed, can you give me some of the details
so that I might be able to straighten them out?

Client: Well, to begin with I have called another travel agency and they
         quoted me a fare that is $100.00 less.

You respond _____

_____

Client: It's March 16 for a one week trip to Costa Rica. But the airfare
         isn't the only problem. The package I reserved was supposed to
         have included a white-water rafting trip. When I went to pay
         the final payment, I was told it did not include the rafting
         trip.

You respond _____

_____

POSSIBLE RESPONSES INCLUDE:

Let me display your record and pull your file, Ms. Kravits. What is the
date of travel and to what destination are you traveling?

I have your file here and it includes a brochure on the package you have
reserved. If the other agency quoted a different price - it might have
been using a different airline, tour company, hotel, or package. Let's
see, your package includes hotel, transfers, city tour, half-day fishing
trip, breakfast daily. The rafting trip is not in the basic package, but
it might have been available as an option. Did you receive a copy of the
brochure describing the package?

This sample call is continued on the next page.

Client: Yes, but I also wrote down what she told me and I have my notes here - it says "rafting trip included."

You respond _____
_____
_____

Client: I don't care what you say, I want the rafting trip included or I am never going to use your travel agency again.

You respond _____
_____
_____

POSSIBLE RESPONSES INCLUDE:

It sounds like there must have been a miscommunication somewhere. Since you would like the rafting trip, let me contact the tour company now and see about including it. If you have a copy of the brochure handy, look on the back of it where the raft trip is shown an option for ....per person. You could also make arrangements for the rafting trip locally and sometimes it is less expensive when booked locally. Many hotels have local tour desks or can direct you to a nearby agency for local trips.

I can understand how upset you are, because when a miscommunication or error is made it can be very aggravating. I can contact the tour company and check if the raft trip option could be discounted for you because of the situation. In addition, please accept our apologies for this inconvenience and we would like to provide you with complimentary travel bags and passport wallets for your trip. Ms. Kravits, I'll call you back in just a few moments after I've talked with the tour company.

KEY POINTS IN HANDLING COMPLAINTS AND IRATE CUSTOMERS

1. Listen to the customer.
2. Empathize with the situation.
3. Tactfully ask questions to determine the errors or mistakes and what (if anything) can be done.
4. Refer it to someone else only after you have made efforts at rectifying the situation.
5. If an apology is called for, be careful enough in your response and what you are apologizing for - to avoid a possible legal issue and subsequent suit.
6. Try to compensate - if it was an error on the agent's/ agency's part.
7. Work with reservation supervisors, sales representatives, or other marketing and managerial staff - if the error was on the part of the tour, cruise or airline company.
8. Keep your voice calm. Do not resort to name-calling. Take a deep breath and think before you speak.
9. If the client gets personal, belligerent, and/or uses foul language, state that you will have to hang up unless a reasonable conversation can take place. If he continues or uses any obscene language, gently hang up and advise the manager.
10. Document facts as discussed. Relate the situation to the manager so that he or she can be aware of it.

62

If possible, repeat the phone call exercise, with an associate acting as the client and your instructor or another person evaluating your performance and skills.

ROLE-PLAY EVALUATION

The first evaluation relates to the agent's approach and greeting:

_____USED CORRECT PHONE ANSWERING/GREETING (identified self, agency)
_____SOUNDED ENTHUSIASTIC (smile in the voice, uplifting tone)
_____SEEMED PROFESSIONAL AND PREPARED (no hesitation, organized)

Then, the agent's attitude and voice qualities:

_____SOUNDED PLEASED	_____SOUNDED NERVOUS	_____SOUNDED BORED
_____VOICE JUST RIGHT	_____VOICE TOO LOUD	_____VOICE TOO SOFT
_____GOOD RHYTHM	_____TALKED TOO FAST	_____TALKED TOO SLOWLY
_____PLEASING VOICE	_____MONOTONE	_____TOO MUCH INFLECTION

Then, the exchange of information:

_____OBTAINED WHO, WHERE, WHEN, TIME PREFERRED, RETURN DATE AND TIME
_____DETERMINED ACCEPTABLE ALTERNATIVES: NON-STOP ONLY, CONNECTIONS, ETC.
_____OBTAINED FARE CONSIDERATIONS, AIRLINE PREFERENCES, ETC.

KEY POINTS RELATING TO SPECIFIC SITUATIONS:

_____PRESENTED SPECIFIC DETAILS AND INFORMATION

_____PRESENTED BENEFITS OF FEATURES

_____USED OPEN-ENDED QUESTIONS (ones that <u>cannot</u> be answered with just "yes" or "no")

_____HANDLED OBJECTIONS

_____DID (OR ARRANGED TO DO) PERTINENT RESEARCH

_____OFFERED TO MAKE TENTATIVE RESERVATIONS AND THEN CONTACT THE CLIENTS TO CONFIRM THEM

_____OBTAINED RESERVATIONS

_____RECOGNIZED BUYING SIGNALS

_____COLLECTED DEPOSIT

_____ANSWERED THE CLIENTS' QUESTIONS (IF ANY)

_____MADE APPROPRIATE RECOMMENDATIONS (IF APPLICABLE)

_____CLOSED THE CALL PROFESSIONALLY/ENDED THE VISIT BY THANKING THE CLIENTS AND ASSURING THEM OF YOUR SERVICES

MAKING RESERVATIONS

Since a travel agent's activities include making reservations for
all types of travel details, the next pages will provide sample
forms for confirmation and sample calls for reservations. The
examples provide practice for:

AIRLINE RESERVATIONS
reservation card example and
calling the airlines information

HOTEL RESERVATIONS
reservation/confirmation form
    and sample call

CAR RENTAL RESERVATIONS
confirmation form and sample call

RAIL RESERVATIONS
reservation form and sample call

then, BASIC STEPS IN SELLING A PACKAGE/TOUR/CRUISE, followed by

PACKAGE/TOUR RESERVATIONS
reservation form and sample call

CRUISE RESERVATIONS
reservation form and sample call

Although the computer may be used for making reservations, you should
practice these calls to become familiar with the details required for
reservations and for calling suppliers if the computer is down.

RESERVATION CARD EXAMPLE

Here is an example of a completed "res" card. This can be used for itinerary planning, as a "backup" for the computer reservation data, or for keeping records.

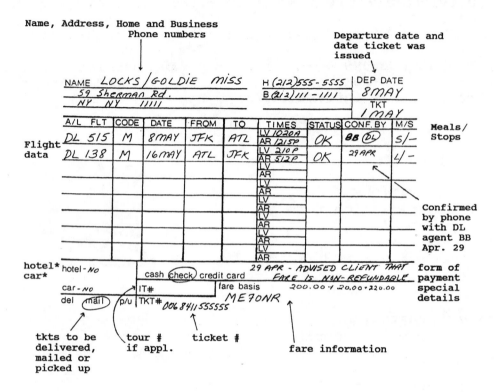

*reservation particulars can be written on the back of the card

NAME _____						H _____		DEP DATE	
_____						B _____			
_____								TKT	

A/L FLT	CODE	DATE	FROM	TO	TIMES	STATUS	CONF. BY	M/S
					LV			
					AR			
					LV			
					AR			
					LV			
					AR			
					LV			
					AR			
					LV			
					AR			
					LV			
					AR			
					LV			
					AR			
					LV			
					AR			

hotel

cash check. credit card

car   IT#   fare basis

del   mail   p/u TKT#

CALLING THE AIRLINES

Be sure to have all necessary information before calling the airlines. If calling for reservations, have flights, names, class of service and other particulars. For domestic airlines reservations, call the first or originating carrier. For international airlines reservations, call the carrier responsible for most of the trip, or particularly the one involved for the international segments.

CALLING THE AIRLINE:

1. Introduce yourself and state why you are calling.

2. If for reservations, give:

   a. airline, flight number

   b. class of service or booking code

   c. day/date

   d. from where to where

   e. how many seats needed

3. After confirmation has been obtained for each flight, verify the fare with the airline and get the reservation agent's name or sine. The airline, in turn, will ask for passenger's name(s) and your ARC or IATA* number.

   NOTE: Use this same format for each flight.

Now look at the sample call provided on the next page.

*International Air Transport Association. Also called IATAN - International Airlines Travel Agency Network.

EXAMPLE OF A CALL FOR AIRLINE RESERVATIONS:

A = AIRLINE RESERVATIONS AGENT

B = TRAVEL AGENT

A: Delta Airlines, may I help you?

B: This is Charmaine from XYZ Travel, calling for reservations.

A: O.K. Go ahead.

B: I need Delta flight number 401, coach class, on October 23, from Tampa to Atlanta, for a party of one.

A: That's confirmed, and the times are 10:20 am to 11:45 am.

B: Then I need the return on Delta flight number 88, coach class, on October 29, from Atlanta to Tampa for the party of one.

A: Confirmed, 6:20 pm to 7:48 pm. Passenger's last name?

B: Rodriguez, R-O-D-R-I-G-U-E-Z, first name John.

A: Your ARC number?

B: 123456; can I please verify the fare?

A: Yes, coach class, round trip, from Tampa to Atlanta is a total of $338.00.

B: O.K. What is your name or sine?

A: My agent's sine is BP, like "be prepared."

B: Thank you.

A: Thanks for calling Delta Airlines.

HOTEL RESERVATION/CONFIRMATION FORM

The top part is used for organizing the information and can be filed for reference. The bottom portion can be detached and used for a request for confirmation (highlight the CONFIRMED BY area for the hotel to complete and ask for a confirmation of the rate). A carbon copy or photocopy should be retained by the agency if mailed and copies can also be given to the client if necessary.

```
CLIENT NAME_____       TODAY'S DATE_____
ADDRESS_____
CITY/STATE/ZIP_____        HOME PHONE_____
                                       BUS. PHONE_____

Any hotel/hotel chain(s) preferred?_____

 Price range ____$35-55 ____$55-75 ____$75-95 ____$95-105 ____$105-125

Location preferred ____city center ____resort area ____shopping area
    ____near airport ____convenient to public transportation
    other_____

Amenities desired ____golf ____tennis ____pool ____beach ____sauna
____exercise room ____nightclub ____restaurant ____24 hr. coffee shop
____meeting rooms ____parking ____handicapped facilities ____shops
____children's activities  other_____
```

```
TO:                                    FROM:
  HOTEL NAME_____              FLY AWAY TRAVEL
    ADDRESS_____               111 First St.
CITY/STATE/ZIP_____             Anywhere, OH 55222
                                            (222) 333-4444
PHONE #S_____(toll-free/local)
This is to provide _____, a party of _____,
                        names
                                       OTHER SPECIFICS:
with a _____type room.  _____
         single, double, etc.

IN DATE_____  OUT DATE_____  TOTAL NIGHTS=_____

RATE OF_____  ARRIVAL TIME _____

SPECIAL CONDITIONS OR GUARANTEE_____

CONFIRMED BY_____ CONF.#_____DATE_____
```

HOTEL DEPOSIT/TOUR/CRUISE/OTHER PAYMENT VOUCHER:

```
Enclosed please find CHECK #_____/MCO#_____
for _____(USD/_____), for payment of the following:
      amount      currency code*
CLIENTS_____ ARRIVAL_____
SPECIFICS_____

TO:                          FROM:    FLY AWAY TRAVEL
                                       111 First St.
                                       Anywhere, OH 55222
                                       (222) 333-4444
```

*cross out "USD" and insert code if another currency applies

Copyright Claudine Dervaes

EXAMPLE OF A CALL FOR HOTEL RESERVATIONS:

A = HOTEL RESERVATIONS AGENT

B = TRAVEL AGENT

A: The Outrigger Inn...Reservations, may I help you?

B: Yes, please. This is Sharon from Let's Be Traveling in Tompson, Missouri, calling for reservations.

A: Fine, what stay dates and accommodations did you need?

B: I need to make reservations for a party of two, Mr. and Mrs. Bill Lewis, for a double room, for two nights, in on August 2 and out on August 4.

A: Just a moment, please. Yes, I can confirm that double for Aug. 2-4 for Mr. and Mrs. Bill Lewis.

B: Thank you. What would be the rate on the room, and what is the applicable tax?

A: The rate is $78.00 per night, plus 8% hotel tax. Will your clients be arriving before 6 p.m.?

B: Yes, they will probably arrive around 3 p.m. May I have your name and a confirmation number if possible?

A: My name is Jeremy, and the confirmation number is 1222444. I need your agency name and address*.

B: This is Sharon, from Let's Be Traveling, 200 East 1st St., Tompson, MO 69988. Our phone number is 333-222-5555.

A: Thank you, did you need anything else?

B: No, not at this time, thank you.

A: Thank you for calling the Outrigger Inn. Have a good day!

B: Thank you. Goodbye.

*some hotels will ask for your ARC or IATA number instead of the address information.

CAR RENTAL RESERVATION FORM

Name(s)_____ Company_____

Address_____ Address_____

City/State/Zip_____ City/State/Zip_____

Phone_____ Phone_____

1ST CAR RENTAL COMPANY:_____PHONE_____

PICK UP CITY_____ LOCATION_____ DATE_____

ARRIVAL TIME AND FLIGHT_____

DROP OFF CITY_____ LOCATION_____ DATE_____

TOTAL DAYS OF RENTAL_____ CLASS AND TYPE OF CAR_____

MAJOR CREDIT CARD_____ SUFFICIENT AGE AND VALID DRIVER'S LICENSE?_____

SPECIAL INFORMATION_____

RATE_____CONFIRMATION NUMBER_____

IF APPLICABLE, PREPAYMENT DETAILS_____

IF APPLICABLE:
2ND CAR RENTAL COMPANY:_____PHONE_____
PICK UP CITY_____ LOCATION_____ DATE_____
ARRIVAL TIME AND FLIGHT_____
DROP OFF CITY_____ LOCATION_____ DATE_____
TOTAL DAYS OF RENTAL_____ CLASS AND TYPE OF CAR_____
MAJOR CREDIT CARD_____ SUFFICIENT AGE AND VALID DRIVER'S LICENSE?_____
SPECIAL INFORMATION_____
RATE_____CONFIRMATION NUMBER_____
IF APPLICABLE, PREPAYMENT DETAILS_____

IF APPLICABLE:
3RD CAR RENTAL COMPANY:_____PHONE_____
PICK UP CITY_____ LOCATION_____ DATE_____
ARRIVAL TIME AND FLIGHT_____
DROP OFF CITY_____ LOCATION_____ DATE_____
TOTAL DAYS OF RENTAL_____ CLASS AND TYPE OF CAR_____
MAJOR CREDIT CARD_____ SUFFICIENT AGE AND VALID DRIVER'S LICENSE?_____
SPECIAL INFORMATION_____
RATE_____CONFIRMATION NUMBER_____
IF APPLICABLE, PREPAYMENT DETAILS_____

NOTES:_____

EXAMPLE OF A CALL FOR CAR RENTAL RESERVATIONS:

A = CAR RENTAL RESERVATIONS AGENT

B = TRAVEL AGENT

A: Drive Away Car Rental...Reservations, may I help you?

B: Yes, please. This is Martha from Traveling Fancy in Podunk, Maine, calling for reservations.

A: Yes, Martha, what city, arrival date and type of car?

B: Las Vegas, Nevada, on April 23, arrival at 10:20 a.m., rental for five days, requesting your least expensive type car. Pick up and return at Las Vegas airport.

A: Just a moment, please. For Las Vegas on April 23 for five days we show that our least expensive car would be a Dodge Colt, 4-door, which is confirmed at a weekly rate of $139.95, unlimited mileage. May I have the last name, please?

B: Last name is Akins, Mr. Charles. Can you tell me what is the rate of tax and if there is an airport access fee?

A: Yes, there is an airport access fee of $3.00 (one time), tax is 7%. Please advise the client to return the car with the same amount of gas as when picked up, and that collision damage waiver insurance is extra. What major credit card will be used?

B: My client will use a Visa.

A: The reservation is confirmed for Mr. Charles Akins, arrival in Las Vegas 10:20 a.m. on April 23, an economy car, unlimited mileage, $139.95 weekly rate, confirmation number is XYZ5551. Your agency's ARC number, please?

B: 123789.

A: Thank you, did you need any additional reservations?

B: No, not at this time, thank you.

A: Thank you for calling the Drive Away Car Rentals. Have a good day!

B: Thank you. Goodbye.

RAIL RESERVATION FORM

Name(s)_____ Adults____ Children____ Ages_____

Address_____ Total passengers = _____

If necessary,

City/State/Zip_____ PASSPORT #(S)_____

Phone_____ _____

RAIL COMPANY:_____PHONE_____

TYPE OF PASS (if appl.)_____ CLASS_____ COST_____
OR
RAIL TICKET
FROM_____ TO_____ DATE_____

TRAIN NAME/NUMBER_____ CLASS_____ SEAT RESERVATIONS_____

SLEEPING ACCOMMODATIONS?_____RESERVED_____COST_____

FACILITIES: Air-conditioned?____ Dining Car?____ Bar?_____ OTHER_____

SCHEDULE:_____

_____

COST_____ RESERVATION #_____ CONFIRMED BY_____ DATE_____

SPECIAL INFORMATION_____

PAYMENT COLLECTED_____ FORM OF PAYMENT_____ DATE_____

DATE TICKETS RECEIVED_____ NET AMOUNT_____ INVOICE#_____SENT_____

TICKETS CHECKED_____ DATE GIVEN/SENT TO CLIENT_____

NOTES:_____

_____

IF APPLICABLE:
2ND RAIL TICKET
FROM_____ TO_____ DATE_____
TRAIN NAME/NUMBER_____ CLASS_____ SEAT RESERVATIONS_____
SLEEPING ACCOMMODATIONS?_____
FACILITIES: Air-conditioned?____ Dining Car?____ Bar?_____ OTHER_____
SCHEDULE:_____
_____
COST_____ RESERVATION #_____ CONFIRMED BY_____ DATE_____
SPECIAL INFORMATION_____
PAYMENT COLLECTED_____ FORM OF PAYMENT_____ DATE_____
DATE TICKETS RECEIVED_____ NET AMOUNT_____ INVOICE#_____SENT_____
TICKETS CHECKED_____ DATE GIVEN/SENT TO CLIENT_____

EXAMPLE OF A CALL FOR RAIL RESERVATIONS:

A = RAIL RESERVATIONS AGENT

B = TRAVEL AGENT

A: French National Railroad...Reservations, may I help you?

B: Yes, please. This is Karen from Let's Go Traveling in Atlanta, and I am calling to order a Eurailpass.

A: What is the client's name and the type of pass you need?

B: I need a 15 day first class Eurailpass for Ms. Kimberly Farina, F-A-R-I-N-A, first name, K-I-M-B-E-R-L-Y, who is leaving for France on July 15.

A: One 15 day first class Eurailpass is confirmed for Ms. Farina; the cost is $225.00. Your agency's name, address, and phone number* please?

B: Let's Go Traveling, 141 North Peachtree, Atlanta, GA 33333, (404) 555-5555.

A: Thank you, we will mail the pass with the invoice right away. Can I help you with any additional reservations?

B: No, not at this time, thank you. Can you provide a pocket schedule book and map showing the train routes and applicable Eurail services?

A: Of course, we will be glad to include the map and pocket guide to schedules with the pass. Would you also like some additional Eurailpass brochures?

B: Yes, please. May I also have your name please?

A: My name is Francois. Thank you for calling the French National Railroad. Have a good day!

B: Thank you. Goodbye.

*some reservations departments will ask for your ARC or IATA number instead of the address information.

BASIC STEPS IN SELLING A PACKAGE/TOUR/CRUISE

Client comes in or calls to inquire about a trip:

AGENT ASKS: Names, # in party, possible dates, destinations, budget considerations, etc. If possible, fill out **Traveler's Profile Form.**

IF DEPARTURE IS MORE THAN SEVERAL MONTHS AWAY...

Agent provides preliminary information, gives or sends to client three or four brochures (based on information obtained from client). Encourages the client to reserve early and may make tentative reservations if a peak/holiday departure is involved. Makes a date to contact the client about the plans and advises the client to call if he/she has any questions or needs further information.

IF DEPARTURE IS WITHIN SIX MONTHS...

Agent may choose a particular brochure (based on evaluation of client's needs) and explain in more detail the suggested tour/ cruise and even check for availability or make a tentative reservation.

IF RESERVATIONS ARE CONFIRMED...

Agent covers the details of the itinerary, schedules, payments due with deadlines, helpful hints, and general information. Agent answers questions, highlights the important areas of the brochure for the client (rates confirmed, cancellation penalties, etc.). Agent includes information on travel insurance and other specifics. Agent attaches his/her business card to the brochure or receipts, advises the client to call for any questions, and thanks the client for contacting the agency.

AGENT: Put dates (deadlines for payments, ticketing, etc.) on a calendar or in the "queues" in the computer.

Make a file folder for forms, the brochure, receipts and other documentation.

Tab the folder with client's NAME, DESTINATION/SHIP, DEPARTURE DATE.

Client folders/files are either placed in a central location or at the individual agent's desk for reference. They are usually filed by departure date/month. After the trip has been completed, the folders are filed by last name of the client. Follow up on clients to maintain their interest and consideration.

TRAVELER'S PROFILE FORM   Date:_____

Name_____ Home Phone_____

Address_____ Work Phone_____

City/State/Zip_____Birthdate(optional)_____

Citizenship_____ Do you have a valid passport?_____

Your profession or business?_____About how many trips
do you take a year?_____ How many are out of the country?_____ About what
percent are business trips?_____ What percent are for pleasure?_____

Which areas have you visited?____Florida ____Calif. ____Hawaii ____Alaska
____Mexico ____Canada ____Caribbean ____Cntrl.Amer. ____South America
____Europe ____Africa ____Middle East ____Asia ____Australia/S.Pacific

Name areas that you are interested in traveling to_____

_____

Do you prefer to travel independently or with a group?_____

Do you prefer deluxe, first class or standard accommodations?_____

What do you usually enjoy doing on your vacation? (check any that apply)
____guided tours ____gourmet dining ____good beaches ____sightseeing
____shopping ____nightlife ____relaxing ____meeting people ____events
sports(__golf __tennis __diving __hiking __camping other_____)

What tour companies have you used before?_____

_____ Any comments on them?_____

_____ Have you ever taken a cruise?_____

Would you like to?_____ If you have cruise experience, what ships and areas?

Do you prefer any ships/cruise lines?_____

_____

What is the most you would normally spend per person on your vacation?

__under $1000 __$1000-2000 __$2000-3000 __$3000-4000 __over $4000

Do you have any medical conditions/allergies that should be considered?____

_____
Are there any frequent flyer/traveler programs you would like considered?

_____

Club/organization memberships:_____

PACKAGE OR TOUR RESERVATION FORM

```
Name(s)_____ Citizenship_____
_____ Citizenship_____
Adults_____ Children_____ Ages_____  Any previous tour experiences?_____
If yes, tour companies, destinations, etc._____

_____
Address_____ Phone #(s)_____
City/State/Zip_____

Departure Date_____ Alternative Dates_____ Number of days_____

1st Tour Company:_____ Tour/Pkg.Name_____
    Phone #_____ IT#_____Date(s)_____
Type of accommodations:   Single   Double   Twin   Triple   Quad
__ROH __STD __SUP __DLX __LUX  Additional features_____
Meal Plan _____ Additional items/options_____
Prices _____per person for    ___land only    ___land & air
Additional costs_____per person-due to tour company.

IF LAND ONLY ADD AIR FARE _____  x  no. of pax  = _____

BRIEF DESCRIPTION/CONFIRMATION OF WHAT PACKAGE OR TOUR INCLUDES:_____

_____

WHAT TOUR/PKG. DOES NOT INCLUDE:_____

DEPOSIT AMT._____ OPTION DATE_____ FINAL PMT.DATE_____
CONFIRMED BY_____DATE_____ FINAL PMT.AMOUNT_____
FORM OF PAYMENT_____
```
```
IF APPLICABLE:
2nd Tour Company:_____ Tour/Pkg.Name_____
    Phone #_____ IT#_____Date(s)_____
Type of accommodations:   Single   Double   Twin   Triple   Quad
__ROH __STD __SUP __DLX __LUX  Additional features_____
Meal Plan _____ Additional items/options_____
Prices _____per person for    ___land only    ___land & air
Additional items & costs_____per person
IF LAND ONLY ADD AIR FARE _____  x  no. of pax  = _____
BRIEF DESCRIPTION/CONFIRMATION OF WHAT PACKAGE OR TOUR INCLUDES:_____
_____
WHAT TOUR/PKG. DOES NOT INCLUDE:_____
DEPOSIT AMT._____ OPTION DATE_____ FINAL PMT.DATE_____
CONFIRMED BY_____DATE_____ FINAL PMT.AMOUNT_____
FORM OF PAYMENT_____
```
```
FLIGHTS:_____
_____
_____

NOTES:_____

_____VALID PASSPORT    _____VISAS    _____TOURIST CARD    ____SHOTS

                 DATE_____   DATE_____   DATE MAILED OR
TICKETS RECEIVED/DONE FOR ____TOUR    ____FLIGHTS   GIVEN TO CLIENT_____
TICKET #S_____
____Travel Insurance Forms/Waiver
____Travel Bags/Passport Wallets
____Travel Checklist & Travel Information Sheet

FOLLOW UP:_____
```

Copyright Claudine Dervaes

EXAMPLE OF A CALL FOR TOUR RESERVATIONS:
(Tour includes airfare and land arrangements)

NOTE: Always have the brochure
at hand when calling.

A = TOUR RESERVATIONS AGENT

B = TRAVEL AGENT

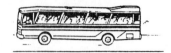

A: Go Getum Tours - Reservations, may I help you?

B: Yes, please. This is Cathy from XYZ Travel in Miami. I need reservations for the Sunspectacular Tour of Mexico, departing April 5.

A: Fine, is it for a party of two requesting a double room?

B: Yes, it is a party of two, Mr. and Mrs. Frank Furter.

A: I can confirm Mr. and Mrs. Frank Furter, double, for Apr. 5 departure of the Sunspectacular Tour, using the Miami gateway.

B: Great. Can you please tell me the flight schedules?

A: Of course. Leaving Miami on April 5, is MX# 344, departing at 11:15 a.m. and arriving in Mexico City at 2:45 p.m. The return from Acapulco is on April 23, MX# 645, departing at 11:52 a.m. and arriving back in Miami at 4:05 p.m. The price of the tour is $1295.00 per person for a total of $2590.00. A deposit of $250.00 is required one week from today and the final payment is due 45 days prior to the departure date.

B: $2590.00 total, and a deposit of $250.00. May I have your name and a confirmation number if possible?

A: My name is Lucy, and the confirmation number is 98973. I need your agency's ARC number. Also, are your clients U.S. citizens and do they have proof of citizenship, preferably passports?

B: Our ARC number is 897654321. And yes, my clients are U.S. citizens and will carry valid U.S. passports. Can you tell me when we can expect the tour documents?

A: Normally the final documents and tickets will be mailed two to three weeks prior to departure. Did you need anything else?

B: No, not at this time, thank you.

A: Thank you for calling Go Getum Tours. Have a good day!

B: Thank you. Goodbye.

CRUISE RESERVATION FORM

Name(s)_____ Citizenship_____

_____ Citizenship_____
Adults_____ Children_____ Ages_____ Any previous cruise experiences?_____

If yes, ships, cruise lines, etc._____

_____

Address_____ Phone #(s)_____

_____
City/State/Zip_____

Departure Date_____ Alternative Dates_____ Number of days_____

1st Cruise Line:_____ Ship_____
      Phone #_____ Sailing Date_____
Cabin Category/#/type requested_____

Confirmed Cabin #_____ Deck_____ Meal Sitting_____

Special Information_____

Prices _____per person for   ___cruise only   ___air sea
Port taxes_____per person. Additional costs_____

DEPOSIT AMT._____ OPTION DATE_____ FINAL PMT.DATE_____

CONFIRMED BY_____DATE_____ FINAL PMT.AMOUNT_____

IF APPLICABLE:
2nd Cruise Line:_____ Ship_____
      Phone #_____ Sailing Date_____
Cabin Category/#/type requested_____

Confirmed Cabin #_____ Deck_____ Meal Sitting_____

Special Information_____

Prices _____per person for   ___cruise only   ___air sea
Port taxes_____per person. Additional costs_____

DEPOSIT AMT._____ OPTION DATE_____ FINAL PMT.DATE_____

CONFIRMED BY_____DATE_____ FINAL PMT.AMOUNT_____

AIR SEA PACKAGE INCLUDES:_____

FLIGHTS:_____

_____

DATE_____   DATE MAILED OR
TICKETS RECEIVED/DONE FOR ____CRUISE ____FLIGHTS GIVEN TO CLIENT_____

OPTIONAL:
____Bon Voyage Gift: _____
____Travel Bags/Passport Wallets
____Travel Checklist
____Cruise Information Sheet
OTHER ITEMS GIVEN TO CLIENT(S)_____

FOLLOW UP:_____

78

EXAMPLE OF A CALL FOR CRUISE RESERVATIONS:

A = CRUISE RESERVATIONS AGENT

B = TRAVEL AGENT

A: West Indies Cruises - Reservations, may I help you?

B: Yes, please. This is Irma from Adventure Travel in Atlanta. I am
    checking for reservations on the Atlantic Odyssey, departing July
    15, requesting cabin category H.

A: Fine, let me check for availability - yes, it is available. I have
    cabin 765 on Sunsplash Deck. Can I have the last names of the
    passengers?

B: Yes, the party of two have the name Hunter, Mr. and Mrs. John.
    They would like first sitting for meals.

A: Confirming Mr. and Mrs. John Hunter, Atlantic Odyssey, July 15,
    and first sitting for meals. The air sea rate is $1895.00 per
    person, plus $33.00 port charges per person. The deposit of $500.00
    is due one week from today; final payment is due six weeks prior.

B: Can you please tell me the flight schedules?

A: Certainly. Leaving Atlanta on July 15 is AA# 543, departing at
    11:15 a.m. and arriving in San Juan at 2:45 p.m. The return
    from San Juan is July 22, departing on AA# 145 at 11:52 a.m.
    and arriving in Atlanta at 4:05 p.m.

B: Thank you. May I have your name and a confirmation number if
    possible?

A: My name is Caroline, and the confirmation number is 43G5R6. What
    is your ARC#?

B: ARC #123456789.

A: Thank you, did you need any additional reservations?

B: No, not at this time, thank you.

A: Thank you for calling West Indies Cruises. Have a good day!

B: Thank you. Goodbye.

ROLE-PLAYING ACTIVITIES

Previous sections of The Travel Training Workbook provided more details, role-play activities and sample conversations. Now, practice these scenarios, using the reservation forms (hotel, tour, cruise, etc.) given on the next pages. For information and specifics and to practice sample calls to suppliers, you should have the following:

> A telephone (unplugged)
> A North American OAG and a Worldwide OAG
> OAG Worldwide Cruise and Shipline Guide (or other cruise
>   references)
> Hotel and Travel Index, OAG Travel Planners, or other
>   hotel references
> Sample brochures from Norwegian Cruise Line, Tauck Tours,
>   or other cruise, tour and package companies (substitute
>   cruise ships or itineraries as necessary)

If resources are unavailable, practice calling the supplier for information. Although the work might be done on a computer, this is good practice for communicating with clients and organizing your presentation. Have the instructor, fellow students, or a third person evaluate your role, using the form provided on the next page. Practice telephone techniques and also practice as if the clients were at your desk (use associates/friends as clients if possible). ADVISE THE EVALUATORS TO USE PENCIL FOR CHECKING THE ITEMS SO THE EVALUATION FORM CAN BE REUSED.

1. Mr. and Mrs. Golden Anniversary want to take a cruise on the S/S Norway. They sailed on it 20 years ago when it was the S/S France. They wish to travel in March and would like an outside cabin on one of the upper decks.

2. Mr. and Mrs. Happy Family and their two children, Biff and Buff, would like to take a trip to Disney World in Orlando. They want to leave early July, for a week to ten days.

3. Mr. Bob Businessman needs air reservations in first or business class from Atlanta to New York and back to Atlanta. He needs to leave tomorrow morning at about 9:00 am and return the following day, leaving around 7:00 pm. He needs an Avis mid-size car rental for pick up and return to the airport. He doesn't need a hotel reservation, since he will be using the company's condominium.

4. Mr. and Mrs. Heavenly Honeymoon want a cruise through the Panama Canal in the first part of November. They would like a deluxe cabin, but they only have $5000.00 to spend.

5. Mr. Wild Guy and Angie Anthropologist want to go to the ruins in the Yucatan Peninsula of Mexico. They are not sure whether they want a tour because they prefer to explore independently and not be confined by an itinerary. They plan to travel in April - for about two weeks.

6. Mr. and Mrs. Elderly would like to take a tour of New England for the fall colors. They would like a fully escorted tour and have heard that a company called Tauck Tours has a good reputation.

80

ROLE-PLAY EVALUATION

The first evaluation relates to the agent's approach and greeting:

_____USED CORRECT PHONE ANSWERING/GREETING (identified self, agency)
_____SOUNDED ENTHUSIASTIC (smile in the voice, uplifting tone)
_____SEEMED PROFESSIONAL AND PREPARED (no hesitation, organized)

Then, the agent's attitude and voice qualities:

_____SOUNDED PLEASED   _____SOUNDED NERVOUS   _____SOUNDED BORED
_____VOICE JUST RIGHT   _____VOICE TOO LOUD   _____VOICE TOO SOFT
_____GOOD RHYTHM   _____TALKED TOO FAST   _____TALKED TOO SLOWLY
_____PLEASING VOICE   _____MONOTONE   _____TOO MUCH INFLECTION

Then, the exchange of information:

_____OBTAINED WHO, WHERE, WHEN, TIME PREFERRED, RETURN DATE AND TIME
_____DETERMINED ACCEPTABLE ALTERNATIVES: NON-STOP ONLY, CONNECTIONS, ETC.
_____OBTAINED FARE CONSIDERATIONS, AIRLINE PREFERENCES, ETC.

KEY POINTS RELATING TO SPECIFIC SITUATIONS:

_____PRESENTED SPECIFIC DETAILS AND INFORMATION

_____PRESENTED BENEFITS OF FEATURES

_____USED OPEN-ENDED QUESTIONS (ones that <u>cannot</u> be answered with
       just "yes" or "no")

_____HANDLED OBJECTIONS

_____DID (OR ARRANGED TO DO) PERTINENT RESEARCH

_____OFFERED TO MAKE TENTATIVE RESERVATIONS AND THEN CONTACT THE CLIENTS
       TO CONFIRM THEM

_____OBTAINED RESERVATIONS

_____RECOGNIZED BUYING SIGNALS

_____COLLECTED DEPOSIT

_____ANSWERED THE CLIENTS' QUESTIONS (IF ANY)

_____MADE APPROPRIATE RECOMMENDATIONS (IF APPLICABLE)

_____CLOSED THE CALL PROFESSIONALLY/ENDED THE VISIT BY THANKING THE
       CLIENTS AND ASSURING THEM OF YOUR SERVICES

81

Use pencil on these forms
so they can be reused.   **CRUISE RESERVATION FORM**

Name(s)_____ Citizenship_____

_____ Citizenship_____
Adults_____ Children_____ Ages_____ Any previous cruise experiences?_____
If yes, ships, cruise lines, etc._____

_____

Address_____ Phone #(s)_____
                                              _____
City/State/Zip_____

Departure Date_____ Alternative Dates_____ Number of days_____

1st Cruise Line:_____ Ship_____
        Phone #_____ Sailing Date_____
Cabin Category/#/type requested_____

Confirmed Cabin #_____ Deck_____ Meal Sitting_____

Special Information_____

Prices _____per person for   ___cruise only   ___air sea
Port taxes_____per person. Additional costs_____

DEPOSIT AMT._____ OPTION DATE_____ FINAL PMT.DATE_____

CONFIRMED BY_____DATE_____ FINAL PMT.AMOUNT_____

IF APPLICABLE:
2nd Cruise Line:_____ Ship_____
        Phone #_____ Sailing Date_____
Cabin Category/#/type requested_____

Confirmed Cabin #_____ Deck_____ Meal Sitting_____

Special Information_____

Prices _____per person for   ___cruise only   ___air sea
Port taxes_____per person. Additional costs_____

DEPOSIT AMT._____ OPTION DATE_____ FINAL PMT.DATE_____

CONFIRMED BY_____DATE_____ FINAL PMT.AMOUNT_____
- -
AIR SEA PACKAGE INCLUDES:_____

FLIGHTS:_____

_____

DATE_____   DATE MAILED OR
TICKETS RECEIVED/DONE FOR ____CRUISE ____FLIGHTS GIVEN TO CLIENT_____

OPTIONAL:
____Bon Voyage Gift: _____
____Travel Bags/Passport Wallets
____Travel Checklist
____Cruise Information Sheet
OTHER ITEMS GIVEN TO CLIENT(S)_____

FOLLOW UP:_____

Copyright Claudine Dervaes

PACKAGE OR TOUR RESERVATION FORM

Name(s)_____ Citizenship_____
_____ Citizenship_____
Adults_____ Children_____ Ages_____ Any previous tour experiences?_____
If yes, tour companies, destinations, etc._____

_____
Address_____ Phone #(s)_____
City/State/Zip_____

Departure Date_____ Alternative Dates_____ Number of days_____

1st Tour Company:_____ Tour/Pkg.Name_____
    Phone #_____ IT#_____Date(s)_____
Type of accommodations: Single   Double   Twin   Triple   Quad
__ROH __STD __SUP __DLX __LUX Additional features_____
Meal Plan _____ Additional items/options_____
Prices _____per person for   ___land only   ___land & air
Additional costs_____per person-due to tour company.

IF LAND ONLY ADD AIR FARE _____ x no. of pax = _____

BRIEF DESCRIPTION/CONFIRMATION OF WHAT PACKAGE OR TOUR INCLUDES:_____

_____

WHAT TOUR/PKG. DOES NOT INCLUDE:_____

DEPOSIT AMT._____ OPTION DATE_____ FINAL PMT.DATE_____
CONFIRMED BY_____DATE_____ FINAL PMT.AMOUNT_____
FORM OF PAYMENT_____

IF APPLICABLE:
2nd Tour Company:_____ Tour/Pkg.Name_____
    Phone #_____ IT#_____Date(s)_____
Type of accommodations: Single   Double   Twin   Triple   Quad
__ROH __STD __SUP __DLX __LUX Additional features_____
Meal Plan _____ Additional items/options_____
Prices _____per person for   ___land only   ___land & air
Additional items & costs_____per person
IF LAND ONLY ADD AIR FARE _____ x no. of pax = _____
BRIEF DESCRIPTION/CONFIRMATION OF WHAT PACKAGE OR TOUR INCLUDES:_____
_____
WHAT TOUR/PKG. DOES NOT INCLUDE:_____
DEPOSIT AMT._____ OPTION DATE_____ FINAL PMT.DATE_____
CONFIRMED BY_____DATE_____ FINAL PMT.AMOUNT_____
FORM OF PAYMENT_____
- -
FLIGHTS:_____
_____
_____

NOTES:_____

_____VALID PASSPORT   _____VISAS   _____TOURIST CARD   ____SHOTS

                    DATE_____   DATE_____   DATE MAILED OR
TICKETS RECEIVED/DONE FOR ____TOUR   ____FLIGHTS   GIVEN TO CLIENT_____
TICKET #S_____
____Travel Insurance Forms/Waiver
____Travel Bags/Passport Wallets
____Travel Checklist & Travel Information Sheet

FOLLOW UP:_____

RESERVATION CARD

NAME _____   H _____   DEP DATE _____
          _____   B _____
          _____   TKT _____

A/L FLT	CODE	DATE	FROM	TO	TIMES	STATUS	CONF. BY	M/S
					LV			
					AR			
					LV			
					AR			
					LV			
					AR			
					LV			
					AR			
					LV			
					AR			
					LV			
					AR			
					LV			
					AR			
					LV			
					AR			

hotel _____   cash check. credit card

car _____   IT# _____   fare basis

del   mail   p/u   TKT# _____

CAR RENTAL RESERVATION FORM

Name(s)_____ Company_____

Address_____ Address_____

City/State/Zip_____ City/State/Zip_____

Phone_____ Phone_____

1ST CAR RENTAL COMPANY:_____PHONE_____

PICK UP CITY_____ LOCATION_____ DATE_____

ARRIVAL TIME AND FLIGHT_____

DROP OFF CITY_____ LOCATION_____ DATE_____

TOTAL DAYS OF RENTAL_____ CLASS AND TYPE OF CAR_____

MAJOR CREDIT CARD_____ SUFFICIENT AGE AND VALID DRIVER'S LICENSE?_____

SPECIAL INFORMATION_____

RATE_____CONFIRMATION NUMBER_____

IF APPLICABLE, PREPAYMENT DETAILS_____

IF APPLICABLE:
2ND CAR RENTAL COMPANY:_____PHONE_____
PICK UP CITY_____ LOCATION_____ DATE_____
ARRIVAL TIME AND FLIGHT_____
DROP OFF CITY_____ LOCATION_____ DATE_____
TOTAL DAYS OF RENTAL_____ CLASS AND TYPE OF CAR_____
MAJOR CREDIT CARD_____ SUFFICIENT AGE AND VALID DRIVER'S LICENSE?_____
SPECIAL INFORMATION_____
RATE_____CONFIRMATION NUMBER_____
IF APPLICABLE, PREPAYMENT DETAILS_____

IF APPLICABLE:
3RD CAR RENTAL COMPANY:_____PHONE_____
PICK UP CITY_____ LOCATION_____ DATE_____
ARRIVAL TIME AND FLIGHT_____
DROP OFF CITY_____ LOCATION_____ DATE_____
TOTAL DAYS OF RENTAL_____ CLASS AND TYPE OF CAR_____
MAJOR CREDIT CARD_____ SUFFICIENT AGE AND VALID DRIVER'S LICENSE?_____
SPECIAL INFORMATION_____
RATE_____CONFIRMATION NUMBER_____
IF APPLICABLE, PREPAYMENT DETAILS_____

THE PSYCHOLOGY OF SELLING

It is important to realize that there is a psychology to selling and having effective sales techniques. The self-assessment should consist of answering and evaluating the questions below:

Am I proud of my profession?

Do I genuinely like myself?

Is there any aspect of selling that makes me uncomfortable?

Can I cope with the rejection that I will inevitably encounter in selling?

The core of self-concept is self-esteem. You must like yourself in order to be liked by other people. And sales are usually based on friendship. People buy from those who have shown an interest and have been sincerely friendly to them. To develop a powerful sales personality, you need both self-esteem and self-confidence. Can you answer "yes" to all the questions below?

Do I have high levels of self-esteem and self-confidence?

Am I determined to succeed?

Do I work towards and attain my goals?

Do I care about my clients and understand their needs?

Do I take responsibility and work hard to achieve success?

Do I believe strongly in my company and my products?

Is it easy for me to make friends with strangers?

Feed your mind with books, tapes, and seminars on sales techniques, time management, motivation, personal development and inspiration. Make a point to read about your profession for 15 minutes a day, and within months you will have read and experienced what might have taken years on the job.

The next important step is understanding why people buy. Evaluate your competencies in this area by reviewing the following:

Do I understand the basic reasons why people buy a product or service?

Do I know how to determine the basic needs of a client?

Do I know the products well enough to make appropriate recommendations?

It is primary to understand that people buy for **their** reasons, not **yours**. A decision to buy means the client will feel better for having made that decision. The client has three choices:

> HE CAN BUY FROM YOU
> HE CAN BUY FROM SOMEONE ELSE
> HE CAN DECIDE <u>NOT</u> TO BUY ANYTHING

Understand the client's needs and emotions, because you need to arouse the DESIRE of the client to own or enjoy the benefits of the product. People buy BENEFITS rather than PRODUCTS, so PERSONALIZE the product's benefits for each customer. For example:

> "Because you enjoy golf and tennis, I think this all inclusive resort hotel with an 18-hole golf course and six tennis courts might offer just the right accommodations and amenities."

To sell effectively also requires the skill of overcoming objections. The best way to respond to an objection is to interpret it as a request for more information. If a client says "I don't think I can go for two weeks" interpret it as "Why should I go for two weeks?" and provide information on alternatives or reasons for the time length.

The proof of effective sales techniques is in the ability to

CLOSE   THE   SALE!

Some specific methods of "closing the sale" are outlined below:

"Kitten Closing" - like holding a kitten, this involves letting the client touch, feel, hold, or try the product. In selling travel, this can mean lending/viewing a video on the cruise/tour/destination or anything that might relate the trip's enjoyment in a "real" way.

"Pro/Con Closing" - get out a piece of paper and on one side you write down favorable reasons for the decision and on the other have the client write down any negative reasons.

"Third Party Closing" - tell the client about other clients who were also hesitant but ended up pleased with the decision.

"Today Only Closing" - it may be the only seat/cabin/room left or the last day the fare may be available.

"Invitational Closing" - ask the client "why don't you give it a try?"

"Six Times Yes Closing" - during the sales presentation ask the client six questions that are sure to obtain "yes" answers. After such confidence, it's hard for the client to say "no."

"Bottom Line Closing" - with the client who is procrastinating, take out all the paperwork and pricing figures and tell him it is a good idea to go ahead with the decision or that he ought to forget it. The client will most likely decide favorably.

THE ABCs OF CLIENTS

A "psychocentric" person wants to travel to local or national places (like Florida, California, New York). An "allocentric" person wants to go to unusual and exotic destinations (India, Indonesia, Papua New Guinea, etc.).

Most people are somewhere in the middle, going to local or national destinations and then later traveling to unusual and far away places. As a travel agent you may handle a wide variety of clients.

<u>Just</u> <u>as</u> <u>examples</u> - below are some "ABCs" of clients and trips -

ANDY ADVENTURE

Independent packages and tours for exploring, safaris, white-water rafting, maybe unusual trips and destinations (South America, Africa, Asia, etc.).

BOB BUSINESS

Air, hotel, car rental - travel requires comfort and convenience, has very specific preferences and needs accurate details (destinations could be anywhere!).

CATHY CULTURE

Tours or independent travel, but wants to go to destinations that offer entertainment, arts, etc. (in U.S. - Boston, New York, Los Angeles, San Francisco, and other major cities; International - Paris, Rome, London, Madrid). However, a client interested in cultures could be budget-constrained/ fascinated by unusual cultures and peoples.

DAN DARING

Windjammer cruises, Club Med vacations, adventure travel.

ED EVENT

Packages to Daytona 500, Mardi Gras, Oberammergau, Superbowl, Wimbledon, you name it.

FRED FAMILY

Packages and possibly cruises (Bahamas, Disneyland/ Disneyworld, Grand Canyon, Niagara Falls, Washington -DC, National Parks, etc.).

HARRY AND HARRIET HONEYMOON

Packages to the Poconos Mountains, Caribbean Island resorts, Hawaii, etc. Maybe a cruise, possibly a trip to Europe.

88

IRMA INEXPENSIVE

Packages and short-length vacations, uses pensions, guest houses, rail passes and other discount vouchers. Travel is to places in the U.S., Mexico, Greece, Turkey, etc.

NANCY NATURE

Specialty tours for environmental causes, trips for bird watching and other outdoor hobbies, maybe safaris to Africa, trips down the Amazon, etc.

PRISCILLA PRIVATE

Has very distinct needs and wants a great deal of attention to the details of seclusion and wants uncommercialized destinations. Maybe a yacht charter, or secluded beach hotel on a island in the Caribbean such as Dominica, Nevis, St. Vincent, etc.

ROBERT RELATIVE

Travel to visit relatives. Airfare only. Probably going to small towns, but may be interested in tracing his Celtic roots and genealogy.

SAMMY SPORTS

Football games, golf tournaments, follows teams, may even organize groups for travel. Destinations could be anywhere.

VERLA VARIETY

A little bit of everything!

WALTER WEALTHY

Uses concorde/first class flights, limousines, and is accommodated in penthouse suites, exclusive castles and chateaux, uses chartered yachts, goes on around the world trips.

IMPORTANT POINTS TO SELLING

1. Since a sale can be made or lost within the first minute of conversation, MAKE SURE YOUR FIRST SENTENCE PROJECTS THE RIGHT ATTITUDE AND INFORMATION.

2. MAKE YOUR CLIENT FEEL IMPORTANT.

3. DON'T JUDGE A CLIENT BY APPEARANCE AND DON'T BE PREJUDICED.

4. ESTABLISH AN APPROPRIATE LEVEL OF COMMUNICATION. Don't use terminology that can confuse, intimidate, or embarrass your client.

5. PUT YOURSELF IN THE CLIENT'S POSITION. Remember that even the smallest journey can be very important to your client, and how you handle the simple arrangement may determine if the client will return for the possible extensive trip.

6. BE A GOOD LISTENER AND CONTROL THE CONVERSATION WITHOUT DOMINATING IT.

7. DON'T KNOCK THE COMPETITION. It will often discourage a client if he hears you "bad mouthing" others. If you happen to gain a customer because he has had a bad experience with a competitor, rely on assuring him that you will do your best to provide professional service and information.

8. ALWAYS CONTROL YOUR TEMPER. Self-discipline and self-control are the marks of a professional and a person who is usually in the right.

9. BUILD AND MAINTAIN ENTHUSIASM.

10. SELL YOURSELF. In every sale it is mostly the PERSON who has succeeded, NOT THE PRODUCT. MAKE YOURSELF A SUCCESSFUL PRODUCT. BELIEVE IN SUCCESS. Don't get discouraged by the sales that are not made, concentrate on those that are.

MARKETING AND SPECIALTY SALES

As presented under "Client Knowledge and Industry Awareness" the travel industry today has increased competition, better educated and more sophisticated travelers, and a wide variety of products. One way to establish or increase the sales and "success" of the agent/agency is to develop a specialty or "niche" area of expertise and sales.

First, examine the markets you want to reach and the specialty area that would be developed in conjunction with that market. Local and national census data, the United States Travel Data Center, and other sources provide research information on the area's demographics.

DEMOGRAPHICS - Statistical information such as age, sex, ethnic background, income, education level, occupation, religion, family status, etc.

Within those statistics, a certain segment can be targeted as a market.

MARKET - A defined group, such as singles, families, seniors, etc.

In addition, with more detailed examination, you can decide to target a specialized sales area such as:

GROUP TRAVEL

SKI VACATIONS

ADVENTURE TRAVEL

BUSINESS TRAVEL

INCENTIVE TRAVEL

TRAVEL FOR THE HANDICAPPED

RELIGIOUS TRAVEL

ENVIRONMENTAL TRIPS

HONEYMOONS

CRUISE TRAVEL

BUDGET TRAVEL

GOLF/TENNIS VACATIONS

The list goes on and on. To specialize in one of the areas listed means that someone assigned or your entire staff must be prepared and professionally equipped to handle the travel specifics. Resources must be available and perhaps discounts or special rates negotiated with the suppliers. The agency should establish an image and suitable decor, or possibly designate an area of the agency specifically for the "niche" sales topic.

The established specialty must then be MARKETED to the clients.

The following advertising media can be used:

TELEPHONE BOOK & YELLOW PAGES

   TRADE AND CONSUMER PUBLICATIONS

      NEWSPAPERS

         MAGAZINES

            DIRECT MAIL (cards, flyers, brochures, newsletters, etc.)

               RADIO

                  TV & VIDEOS

                     OUTDOOR SIGNS

                        BILLBOARDS

                           ELECTRONIC ADVERTISING
(online computer services)

                          PROMOTIONS

                        NOVELTY ITEMS

                         PUBLIC RELATIONS

                        EVENTS

A way to reduce the cost of using some of these mediums is by CO-OP ADVERTISING, which means sharing the advertising costs with a vendor or supplier, or even other agencies.

What colors work best in advertising?

Here are some advantages and disadvantages of colors that can be used:

RED - adds excitement, but overuse can be difficult and tiring to read

BLUE - has a calming effect, but overuse can neutralize your efforts

---

REVIEW

1. Name six "methods" of closing the sale.

   a. _____

   b. _____

   c. _____

   d. _____

   e. _____

   f. _____

2. Name six specialty areas that an agency can target.

   a. _____

   b. _____

   c. _____

   d. _____

   e. _____

   f. _____

3. Define demographics. _____

   _____

4. A defined group, such as families, singles, students, etc. is called
   a _____.

5. Name eight types of marketing media.

   a. _____

   b. _____

   c. _____

   d. _____

   e. _____

   f. _____

   g. _____

   h. _____

GROUP TRAVEL

A travel agency can specialize in or have a group travel department. It can have an appointed staff or person who handles the planning, negotiating, marketing, reservations, payments and operations.

From the agency standpoint, the **ADVANTAGES** of group travel include:

Building a list of clients

Expanding the base of possible future travelers

Offering a large profit potential

Allowing the agency to mark up the product

Diversifying the products to help in weak business periods

From the agency standpoint, the **DISADVANTAGES** of group travel include:

Mistakes can be multiplied

Everything must be geared to the group, not individual desires (less personal than one on one)

Group planning is long term: By the time the trip happens, the agent may not feel the same sense of satisfaction that accompanies a client's trip

More communication skills are required - for contracts, flyers, brochures and other promotional materials

More negotiating skills are required for working with suppliers

Necessary organizational skills are multiplied by the group numbers

Knowledge of the products has to be more complete since the agent/agency is more responsible for the design of the itinerary and trip details

The question arises: Should the agency first obtain a group and then plan the customized tour or plan a customized tour and then market it to a group? The best answer depends on the circumstances, but the agency should really do both. The intial steps would be to look at the types of clients already on the mailing list, the types of clients that could be secured, and the costs of reaching a certain market.

OUTLINE FOR DESIGNING A GROUP TOUR/CRUISE

1. DESIGN THE TRIP CONCEPT.

2. PLAN THE ITINERARY/ITINERARIES - Decide on destinations, types of trips, tour companies, cruise lines/ships, dates, number of departures, etc.

3. RESERVE SPACE AND THE DETAILED ARRANGEMENTS.

4. COST THE COMPONENTS AND PRICE THE TOUR/CRUISE.

5. DESIGN AND PUBLISH THE PROMOTIONAL MATERIALS (FLYERS, BROCHURES, ADVERTISEMENTS, ETC.).

6. MARKET THE TOUR/CRUISE (SEND OUT LITERATURE, DO PROMOTIONAL EVENTS, SEND PRESS RELEASES, RUN ADVERTISEMENTS, ETC.).

7. ESTABLISH INQUIRY/RESERVATIONS OPERATIONS AND DETAILS.

8. SET UP REVIEW DATES AND PERIODICALLY CHECK WITH SUPPLIERS, TOUR GROUP LEADERS/ORGANIZERS.

9. KEEP TRACK OF THE NUMBER OF RESERVATIONS, DEPOSITS AND FINAL PAYMENTS REQUIRED, MANIFEST DEADLINES, ETC.

10. INITIATE ADDITIONAL PROMOTIONS IF NECESSARY AND/OR FOLLOW UP ON INQUIRIES/LEADS THAT HAVE NOT YET BEEN RESERVED.

11. BRIEF THE TOUR ESCORTS/GUIDES (2 to 5 days prior to departure). CHECK ALL TRIP DETAILS. REVIEW ALL CONTRACTS.

12. ADVISE THE TOUR ESCORT/MANAGER TO CONTACT YOU OR A SPECIFIED INDIVIDUAL DURING THE TRIP FOR ANY PROBLEMS.

13. AFTER THE TOUR, REVIEW THE SUCCESSES/PROBLEMS WITH THE ESCORT. ALSO, A DAY OR TWO AFTER THE GROUP HAS RETURNED (a) CONTACT AND WELCOME THEM BACK, (b) SOLICIT THEIR COMMENTS FOR IMPROVEMENTS AND FUTURE TRIPS (USE A QUESTIONNAIRE IF POSSIBLE).

14. COMPLETE A PROFIT/LOSS REPORT ON THE TOUR AND USE ALL PERTINENT REPORTS AND FEEDBACK TO MAKE CHANGES AND DELETIONS FOR FUTURE GROUP TOURS/CRUISES.

GROUP QUESTIONNAIRE

Group Name_____ # of pax_____ Origin_____

Other origins & # of pax_____

Contact Name_____ Address_____

Phone_____ City/State/Zip_____

Has the group ever traveled together before?____ If yes, what dates, destinations,

and details_____

_____

_____

Does the group already have an escort?_____ Does the group also want an escort

from the tour company?_____ Agency?_____ Is the group planning on having the

escort/designated leader travel free?_____ Total complimentary requested_____

Possible dates for tour/cruise_____

Types of packages/tours/cruises_____

Preference of accommodations _____Deluxe ____First class ____Standard

Specifics requested: ____All meals ____breakfast (full/continental_____)
____lunch ____dinner ____cocktail party (cash bar/open bar_____)
____banquet ____wine w/dinner ____flowers ____fruit ____hospitality suite
____travel bags ____English speaking guide/languages needed_____
____deluxe motorcoach ____standard motorcoach ____vans/minibuses ____taxis
____theater tickets ____train tickets ____bus tickets ____sightseeing tickets
____transfers guided sightseeing to_____
____tips included (baggage, meals, etc._____)
____taxes included (hotel, departure, etc._____)

Please provide a detailed outline of the itinerary requested_____
_____
_____
_____
_____
_____

Date quote is needed_____ Will the group assist in promotion?_____ If

yes, how?_____

# of flyers needed_____ # of brochures_____ Other needs_____

NOTES_____

SOME BASIC Q.s & A.s OF GROUP TRAVEL

Q. **WHAT ARE THE ADVANTAGES OF GROUP TRAVEL FOR THE CLIENTS?**

A. The clients can possibly SAVE MONEY by traveling with a group. They can have a sense of COMFORT in being with others of the same interest/background/etc. They have the opportunity of COMPANIONSHIP and making new friends and acquaintances, the CONVENIENCE of having trip details taken care of and less responsibility for decisions and/or problems. Their trip itinerary may be MORE CUSTOMIZED than what would normally be available.

Q. **WHAT ARE THE SOURCES FOR GROUPS?**

A. Sources include: existing clients with their families, friends, clubs, businesses, organizations, etc.; agency employees and their families, friends, organizations; community groups; business and professional groups; church groups; health club groups; and groups of a specific ethnic background, sports or other interest, school/ college, age category, status, etc.

Q. **WHAT ARE SOME DETAILS TO CONSIDER WHEN PLANNING THE TOUR DATES?**

A. Weather, school vacations, holidays, low or peak season airfares/ hotel prices, special promotions going on, the destinations/types of trips that are the latest trend, the potential participants for the tour, and whether you have enough time to promote the tour.

Q. **WHAT SHOULD BE CONSIDERED FOR THE AIRLINE/FLIGHT ARRANGEMENTS?**

A. The use of national airlines vs. U.S. airlines, the reputation and service of the airline, the most convenient schedules, best fares, possible override commissions, discounts, upfront monies required, cooperation, possible assistance in promotion, bonuses (use of airline clubs at airports, gifts, etc.).

Q. **WHAT SHOULD BE CONSIDERED FOR THE LAND ARRANGEMENTS?**

A. The **tour company's** reputation, service, performance, association memberships, default protection, rates, discounts, override commissions, bonuses; the **hotels'** locations, amenities, reputation, service, rates, discounts, commissions, bonuses; the **restaurants'** locations, services, food quality, reputation, cleanliness, prices; trip details such as the **guides'** language abilities (perfect English, etc.), knowledge of the groups' specific interest, experience, number of guides per group; the **transportation details** (type of bus, space, reclining seats, smoking/non-smoking regulations, large windows, toilet facility, air-conditioned/heated, scheduled stops, and the possibility of unscheduled stops).

IMPORTANT POINTS ABOUT THE TOUR ITINERARY, PRICE, AND BROCHURE

When preparing a quote for a group, write out all the details, price it based on the **minimum** number of participants, specify a date the quote is valid until, include a "subject to change" clause - if air fares used may alter, and be sure it is understood that it is a quote for the "approximate" cost, not the final figure.

Once the tour is planned, make sure the format and details are clear, appealing, and professional.

The pace of the tour should be reasonable, not too fast or too slow.

The statements about the tour need to be clear with no room for misinterpretation, misunderstanding or confusion.

The tour brochure and itinerary should highlight the agency's and the group's identity, making it "special."

Pricing should be competitive, but also include a safety margin to cover errors, increases, unforeseen costs.

There should be no doubt about the cost - state what it includes and what it does not include.

Make certain the terms and conditions are explicit and that payment requirements and cancellation policies are specific and reasonable.

RESOURCES FOR SKILLS IN GROUP TRAVEL

Group travel is a very diversified area of the travel industry and includes family reunions, conventional tours, special interest travel, incentive travel, meetings and conventions. Education and training for this specialty area can come from attending seminars and trade shows, reading industry and consumer publications, travel experiences and various references/training manuals. The group travel "expert" can be in planning, sales, marketing, reservations, operations, or perform as the tour guide/escort/manager. The following are some resources for group travel. Check your local library or contact Solitaire Publishing for further information.

The Company Group Manual for Outside Sales and Operations

The Company Tour Escort Manual

Group Travel Operations Manual

Conducting Tours

Building Profits with Group Travel

GROUP TRAVEL - REVIEW

1. Give three **advantages** for the agency specializing in group travel.

   a. _____

   b. _____

   c. _____

2. Give three **disadvantages** for the agency specializing in group travel.

   a. _____

   b. _____

   c. _____

3. Name three advantages of group travel for the clients.

   a. _____

   b. _____

   c. _____

4. Give five of the possible sources for groups.

   a. _____

   b. _____

   c. _____

   d. _____

   e. _____

5. Name four items to consider for the airline and land arrangements.

   AIRLINE CONSIDERATIONS   LAND CONSIDERATIONS

   a. _____   a. _____
      _____   _____

   b. _____   b. _____
      _____   _____

   c. _____   c. _____
      _____   _____

   d. _____   d. _____

OUTSIDE SALES

One of the marketing and sales techniques used by travel agencies is to hire outside sales people. The outside salespersons usually work on a commission basis.

For example: If the agency earns $43.18 (10%) on the airline fare of $431.81, the outside agent working on 2% earns $8.63. Some agencies will state compensation as a percentage of **their** commission - the outside agent working on 20% earns $8.63 ($43.18 X 20%).

Below are some of the different areas of outside sales promotion with sample levels of commission and compensation.

OUTSIDE SALES AGENTS for:

COMMERCIAL ACCOUNTS
Starting commission at 2%, increase to 5% based on volume of business. On accounts that are retained year to year, the commission percentage drops. Agency employer sets goals for commercial account volume and evaluates the quality of the account.

ACTIVITIES INCLUDE: Call on businesses and corporations and meet with travel managers and travel decision makers. Complete Profile Forms on travelers (see next page). Present travel agency kit outlining services and specifics. Follow up with appointments for detailing travel policies, special supplier arrangements, and continuing communication.

GROUP TRAVEL
Compensation varies. Some outside agents for group travel are compensated by traveling free of charge with the group. The agent accompanying the group may act as the tour escort and receive tips from the group. If the outside agent solicits and organizes the operations, the compensation may be a salary, a salary plus commission for a certain volume, a split commission, or a split commission plus bonuses for certain volume amounts.

ACTIVITIES INCLUDE: Call on groups, clubs, associations, and other contacts. Complete group questionnaire. Work with group leader or contact on trip details and promotion. May also plan itinerary, negotiate prices, reserve space, handle reservations, payments and ticketing. May also put on "cruise night" and tour promotions, events, and handle mailings.

BUSINESS TRAVELER PROFILE FORM

NAME_____ TITLE_____

COMPANY_____ PHONE_____

ADDRESS_____ CITY/STATE/ZIP_____

CITIZENSHIP_____ VALID PASSPORT____ HOME PHONE_____

RESERVATIONS ARE NORMALLY MADE BY ___SECRETARY - NAME_____

___MYSELF   ___TRAVEL MANAGER - NAME_____

Trip information can be given to ___secretary ____spouse Other_____

Regular destinations include:_____

Infrequently travel to:_____

Possibility of travel to:_____

Preferred Airlines   Frequent Flyer Numbers   Other information

_____
_____
_____
_____
_____

Class of Service preferred   ___First Class ___Business Class ___Coach Class
Seating Preferred ___Aisle ___Window ___Bulkhead ___Non-smoking ___Smoking
  Other particulars_____
Dietary needs_____

I prefer   ___non-stop ___direct ___changing planes if less expensive

Exceptions_____

Considerations:____100% penalties OK ____Prefer no penalty ____Some penalty OK

Exceptions_____

Preferred Car Rental   Account Numbers   Type of car and other information
_____
_____
_____

Preferred Hotels   City   Other Information
_____
_____
_____
_____

                                              For agency use:
Credit Cards   Numbers   Expiration   Signature on File
_____
_____
_____
_____
_____

Emergency information/contact:_____
_____

LEISURE TRAVEL

For referral only, the commission may be 1% - 3%.
In some cases compensation is a flat fee - $5.00 for
leisure travel referral, $20.00 for a business. If
the outside agent finds the account and makes the
reservations, the commission could be 3% - 5%, and
may include bonuses for volume or particular vendors.
If the outside sales agent handles all the services,
the compensations may be 5% - 7% and again volume or
preferred suppliers may increase the amount.

ACTIVITIES INCLUDE: Call on friends, relatives, business
contacts, clubs, groups, social gatherings, apartment
complexes and all other possible travelers. Complete
traveler's profile forms. May organize trip details,
make reservations, handle payments and ticketing.

INCENTIVE TRAVEL*

Compensation varies from 2% - 5% plus bonuses for
volume.

ACTIVITIES INCLUDE: Call on businesses and corporations
and meet with travel managers and travel decision makers.
Complete a profile on the employers/employees' interests,
budget, previous programs, proposed theme and inclusions.
Go over details, outline and strategies of promotion,
evaluation and specifics. Follow up with appointments for
travel awards presentation and cruise/tour operation.

Many times the outside sales agents handle more than one area of
sales and they also may specialize in an area such as cruises,
student travel, adventure travel, etc.

How can an agency find outside sales agents? Run advertisements, ask
the existing employees for suggested contacts, review any prospective
employees, contact travel schools, research your client files, contact
retired persons, or past group leaders. Another method is to hold a
seminar or presentation to acquire names of people who might be
interested.

Because of the significant liability and investment of time that can
result from using outside sales agents, it is a good idea to:

THOROUGHLY INTERVIEW THE APPLICANT
DRAW UP A CONTRACT
ENCOURAGE TRAINING AND SUPERVISE THEIR BOOKINGS
CONTINUE TO MOTIVATE

*Travel as a reward for sales or work done by employees of companies.

STEPS IN HIRING OUTSIDE SALES AGENTS

COMPLETE A THOROUGH INTERVIEW and ask a lot of questions -
Do they have a market? What contacts do they have (be specific)?
Can they produce enough volume to make it worthwhile for both
of you? Do they have any training or travel skills? Are they
professional and qualified to represent your business? Have
they worked with another agency? Can they produce a marketing
plan?

IF HIRED, DRAW UP A CONTRACT (see the sample provided in this manual).
There are many reasons to have a contract. It protects both the
agency and the outside agent from misunderstanding. It can be
used for verifying the activities of the outside agent for
travel industry benefits. Growth potential can also be spelled
out in contracts. And most importantly, the contract can help
verify if the status of the outside agent is an independent
contractor or an employee. If the agent is deemed an employee
by the state and federal authorities, the agency has significant
liability for paying taxes, minimum wages, overtime, etc.

ENCOURAGE THEIR TRAINING in the basics of agency operations. Sell
them (for $1.00) back issues of references, training manuals,
and encourage them to ask questions. Possibly give them a bonus
for attending seminars and conferences.

SUPERVISE the bookings, payments, etc. Have an agent in the office
review items to make sure there are no errors. It is a good
idea to have a "buddy" system for the outside sales agent.

MOTIVATE them continually. Do periodic reviews (semi-annual, annual).
Set performance levels. Congratulate them on jobs well done.
Provide incentives for increased sales. Circulate pertinent
familiarization trip, seminar, trade show, and other industry
offers to them. Make sure the inside and outside agents work
effectively and cooperatively and that there are no "hard
feelings" between the two. Look for any problems and work on
solutions so that all the staff are coordinated and cohesive.

EMPLOYEE VS. INDEPENDENT CONTRACTOR

AN EMPLOYEE

Is under another's control for what is accomplished and is controlled as to the details and the means by which it is accomplished.

Can be fired (discharged).

Is furnished with tools, materials, supplies, and equipment.

Is furnished a place to work.

Is required to comply with instructions as to how, when and where to work.

Receives training.

Performs activities which are closely integrated with the claimed employer's business.

Has a set time to work.

Has expenses reimbursed.

Must perform services personally.

Has an ongoing relationship with the claimed employer.

Has restraints for working with others now or after being discharged from the current claimed employer.

Except for the first item indicated, no one single factor is a final determinant.

AN INDEPENDENT CONTRACTOR

Is engaged in independent employment and controls what is accomplished and how it is accomplished.

Furnishes the supplies and equipment needed, as well as the place to work.

Pays any expenses.

Offers services to other businesses or the public.

Has the specialized knowledge to do the work.

Sets the hours for work.

May delegate work to his/her own assistants.

Is paid on a straight commission basis.

Has the opportunity to make a profit or suffer a loss.

Must complete the work that has been contracted.

Pays self-employment taxes.

Except for the first item indicated, no one single factor is a final determinant.

INDEPENDENT CONTRACTOR AGREEMENT

The contract below is for example only. Have an attorney review any
contracts or documents before using.

DATE_____
AGREEMENT BETWEEN XYZ TRAVEL, INC. AND _____.
XYZ TRAVEL, INC. is an ARC appointed agency providing airline tickets, travel
reservations and other documentation and has a reputation for fair dealing with
the public. XYZ Travel, Inc. has an office in Podunk, MO and is properly equipped
to handle the services for selling travel.
XYZ Travel, Inc. has deemed that it will be to the mutual advantage of XYZ Travel,
Inc. and _____ to enter into the following agreement.
_____agrees to provide fair dealing and proper services in
selling travel to customers for XYZ Travel, Inc.
_____shall be paid a commission for travel sales accepted and
completed by XYZ Travel, Inc. Such commissions shall be _____% for_____
_____.
The commission payments shall be made only after the customers' travel has been
completed.
XYZ Travel, Inc. agrees that, because its business will require the use of certain
stationery and forms, it will provide _____ with needed supplies
for such services.
_____shall be liable for all expenses which will include, but
not be limited to, telephone calls, bank debits for returned checks, ticket delivery
etc. XYZ Travel, Inc. shall not be liable to _____ or any third
party for any of _____'s acts.
_____shall not have the authority to bind, obligate or commit
XYZ Travel, Inc. by any promise or representation unless specifically authorized in
writing by XYZ Travel, Inc.
In the event any transaction in which_____is involved results
in a dispute, litigation, or legal expenses, the independent contractor shall be
liable for all expenses connected with the dispute.

XYZ Travel, Inc. maintains the right to contract for similar services with other
individuals and/or businesses.

_____agrees to perform the services on each sale accepted in a
manner in accord with the format which may be prescribed or regulations applicable
to the sale and in a manner in accord with ordinary business custom.

This agreement does not constitute a hiring by either party. The parties of this
agreement shall remain independent contractors bound by the provisions stated.
_____is NOT under the control of XYZ Travel, Inc. as to the
result of what is accomplished, nor the means and details of how it is accomplished.
This agreement shall not be construed as a partnership, and neither party shall be
liable for any obligations incurred by the other except by the provisions outlined
in this agreement. XYZ Travel, Inc. shall not make any premium payments or contri-
butions for _____for any workmen's compensation or unemployment
compensation. _____agrees to be responsible for all federal
and state income taxes and social security taxes.

This agreement and the relationship created by this agreement may be terminated by
either party, with or without cause, at any time, with 14 days written notice to
the other party. Upon termination of this agreement,_____agrees
not to furnish any person, firm, or company engaged in a competitive business any
information as to XYZ Travel, Inc.'s customers, prices, terms, or other information.
This agreement shall be governed by the laws of the state of Missouri.
Witness the signatures of the parties, as agreed on the stated date and year.

_____   _____ Date_____
President, XYZ Travel, Inc.   witness

_____   _____ Date_____
Outside Agent   witness

OTHER POINTS ABOUT OUTSIDE SALES

Outside sales agents need to carefully log their contacts and activities for follow up with the travel agency. The accountability of both the agent and the agency is handled by the use of forms. Forms give a record of what has been done, what is to be done, and what should be done on a continual basis. Some forms that can be used by outside agents are:

> Weekly Call Report
> Sales Lead Sheets
> Traveler's Profile Forms
> Group Questionnaire
> Business Traveler Profile Form
> Incentive Travel Prospect Report

Outside sales agents have to be very self-motivated, aggressive, out-going, personable, neat, and sales-oriented. Travel agency experience is helpful, but not required. Outside agents should have many contacts (groups, businesses, friends) or be able to make many contacts for travel sales opportunities.

Normally, outside agents should be able to gross at least $70,000 a year in order to be worthwhile for both the agent and the agency. In some cases, the agency may set much higher goals.

In order to establish the outside sales agent as an independent contractor, agencies can "rent a desk" - charging an amount for use of the desk, computer, phone, etc. A token amount can be assessed ($5.00 a month) or a larger amount can be charged in connection with higher commissions paid to the outside agent.

As independent contractors, the outside sales agents should pay for any familiarization trips and other expenses.

In some states, outside sales agents may need to register as a "travel promoter." Contact the state's Department of Consumer Services for clarification of restrictions and policies.

Note that different contracts can be negotiated with the outside sales agents - depending on their marketing specialty and desired benefits.

The travel privileges for the outside sales agents can be stated in the contract.

The outside sales agents should receive a copy of the agency's office procedures manual.

For insurance coverage the agency can add a rider to its policy for the outside sales agents (outside agents pay the premiums).

It is a good idea to obtain a determination letter from the Internal Revenue Service as to the status of employees versus independent contractors.

A COMPARISON

OUTSIDE SALES AGENT	VS.	INSIDE SALES AGENT
flexible schedule		fixed schedule
can work at home		works at an office
doesn't have to sit at a desk		mostly sits at a desk
helpful to have many contacts		not as necessary to have contacts
doesn't require as detailed training in all areas		requires detailed training in all areas
sometimes an entry job for travel school graduates		difficult to start unless training was very thorough
good for those with "sales experience" or no "travel job experience"		requires travel job experience or thorough travel training
gives formal sales presentations and makes cold calls		no formal sales presentations are usually necessary
self-motivated to make sales calls		motivated, but clients are contacting the agency
outgoing and aggressive		helpful to be outgoing
good for retired persons, or for part-timers (for some specialty areas)		open to anyone who has the capabilities
compensation can be in the form of benefits instead of pay		usually working to earn a living
good if agent is "burned out" from inside sales		good if agent is "burned out" from outside sales

These are generalizations only.

REVIEW ON OUTSIDE SALES

1. Outside sales agents usually work on a _____ basis.

2. Different specialty areas can be handled by outside sales agents, such as _____, _____, _____, and _____.

3. It is important for the agency to determine the status of the outside sales agents, designating them as _____ or _____.

4. Name three items that determine the agent is an **employee**.

   a. _____

   b. _____

   c. _____

5. Name three items that determine the agent is an **independent contractor**.

   a. _____

   b. _____

   c. _____

MEETING PLANNING AND MANAGEMENT

Meeting planning and management is an incredibly complex type of travel planning and one that requires tremendous attention to organization, details, and the particular corporations or businesses involved. Many meeting planners work on agreed upon fees rather than commissions.

Meeting Planners International (MPI) and the American Society of Association Executives (ASAE) are two of the organizations that can assist with networking and learning opportunities. Meeting News, Successful Meetings, Business Travel News magazines, Networld, the Official Meetings and Facilities Guide, Nationwide Intelligence - these are just some of the many resources for meeting planners.

There are several steps to planning a meeting:

KNOW THE OBJECTIVES - - - -
What is the premise of the meeting and what is it supposed to accomplish? Is it an educational symposium? A social event? A motivational presentation? An awards ceremony?

ESTABLISH THE PARAMETERS - - - -
How many attendees estimated? How many sleeping rooms? Will reservations be made through you or directly with the hotel?

PLAN THE PROGRAM - - - -
Prepare a daily schedule of activities and determine the meeting space and banquet requirements. The agenda should list each function and event that will take place - seminars, meetings, meals and breaks, receptions, trade shows, banquets, sporting events, free time, transportation, any sightseeing activities, etc. Try to vary the types of formats so that the meeting is more enjoyable and interesting.

PREPARE THE BUDGET - - - -
Consider all the charges: meeting rooms, food and beverages, taxes, tips, support and promotional materials, printing, postage, labor, telephone expenses, speaker fees, costs for transportation, banners and signs, badges and gifts, audio/visual aids and other items. Allocate an additional 5% to 10% for unforseen charges. Allow for revenues from the registration fees, sponsorships, and any exhibitor fees.

SELECT A SITE - - - -

Consider where the attendees will come from, the
number of sleeping rooms and meeting rooms you
will need, and the hotel amenities the attendees
may need or want. There are many different types
of meeting locations to choose from:
airport hotels, resort areas, suburb hotels,
convention centers, downtown hotels, colleges,
cruise ships, and even outdoor parks
and recreation areas.
Use the various resources as well as contact the
convention/tourist bureau for assistance.

WORK WITH THE HOTEL/SITE - - - -

Make a list of the contact people. This includes
the sales manager, convention services manager,
general manager, caterer, meeting facilities
manager, food and beverage director, front office
manager, reservations manager, housekeeping supervisor, audio/visual technician, etc. Go over a
fire and safety checklist. Negotiate the contracts.

ORGANIZE THE AIR AND GROUND TRANSPORTATION DETAILS - - - -

Determine the airline(s) to consider and possibly
designate an "official" carrier. Negotiate the
fares and details. Benefits to consider including
are provided later in this section. You may decide
to use a Destination Management Company (DMC) to
handle the ground transportation.

PROMOTE THE MEETING/CONFERENCE - - - -

Flyers, letters, brochures, press releases,
advertising in trade publications - these are all
part of the promotion.

ORGANIZE THE MEETING DETAILS - - - -

Posters, banners, signs, name badges, exhibitor
signs, room(s) setup, audio/visual equipment,
food and beverages, banquets and special events
or presentations - review all the procedures and
the scheduled time frames. As a rule of thumb,
plan to have at least one staff member for every
50 attendees. Work out the amenities and details
for VIPs and other special guests. The on-site
meeting staff should arrive at least one day
prior to the program. The staff's rooms should
all be located on lower floors and in the same
area to make it convenient for updates and
organizational meetings. Familiarize the staff
with the hotel's rooms, registration areas, etc.

FINAL DETAILS - - - -

Check reservations, have a pre-conference meeting, review the entire program, go over registration procedures, work out a communications center, remain close and in a supervisory capacity, observe how meeting events are proceeding, make immediate corrections if necessary. At the end of each day, go over the next day's program and incorporate any changes you find important.

AFTER THE MEETING - - - -

Evaluate the meeting, facilities, food, rooms, services, etc. Record the evaluations of the attendees and make notes of what should be changed for the next meeting. Send thank-you notes to hotel staff that were particularly helpful and possibly provide extra gratuities to the Bell Captain, Housekeeping, Banquet Manager, etc.

SAMPLE MEETING PLAN SHEET

COMPANY: *Carson Chemicals*   CONTACT: *Phillip Morrison*

EVENT: *Awards Banquet*   DATE: *April 5, 1993*

SIGN AS: *CarsonChem Awards*   ROOM & TIME: *Oak - 6:00 p.m.*

OF PAX: *64*   SETUP: *8 tables for eight*

A/V: *lectern with microphone*

FOOD & BEV.: *open bar from 6:00 pm to 7:00 pm*
7:00 pm dinner buffet (see attached menu)

OTHER: *one six foot draped table next to lectern*

DATE PREPARED *October 10, 1992*   by *Cathy Crosby*

PAGE *3* OF *5*

Experienced meeting planners and travel managers recognize that there are many aspects to the details of meetings and conferences. Since one of the main points is the area of NEGOTIATION, the next page outlines some of the particulars that can be discussed and agreed upon with the airlines and the hotels selected.

Negotiable <u>AIRLINE</u> <u>BENEFITS</u> include:

*Complimentary or reduced rate tickets for meeting staff used for site selection, pre-conference organization trips, etc.

*Complimentary seats for staff accompanying the group (usually one for every 15 members)

*Waiving restrictions on promotional fares, extra discounts on promotional fares (usually 5%)

*Blocks of seats, allowing the group members to be seated together

*Promotional assistance such as mailing shells, co-op advertising, etc.

*Single invoice billing for all tickets, regardless of originating point

*Special amenities such as free beverages, group welcome, customized gifts, use of airline club lounges at airports, early boarding, welcome banners, first-off passengers and baggage handling, and ground transportation

*Freight assistance and special rates for shipping meeting materials and equipment

*Assistance with planning, site research, and dedicated phone lines to provide information and take reservations

Negotiable <u>HOTEL</u> <u>BENEFITS</u> include:

*Special rates for rooms, meals, meeting rooms

*Special check-in desk and personnel

*Late check-out time or early check-in times

*Airport transfers

*Welcome cocktail party and reception

*Hospitality suites

*Morning newspapers, nightly turn-down service

*Wine, fruit, flowers, or gifts delivered to rooms

*Free parking

*Complimentary rooms for meeting staff during site inspection and for conference.

QUESTIONS TO ASK AND ITEMS TO OBTAIN FROM THE CATERER INCLUDE:

Contact name for planning_____

Contact name during function_____

Obtain the menus with prices. Are you limited to the menus? If not,
    is it possible to create your own menu?

What are the caterer's specialties?

Which entrees are fresh? Frozen?

Are vegetables fresh or canned?

What size portions are served at lunch? Dinner?

Is there complimentary coffee? Tea?

Are substitutions allowed for those on special diets? How much advance
    notice is required?

How much time should be allowed for meals?

What is the waitperson to attendees ratio?

When must guarantees be final?

When is payment due?

What is the sales tax? Gratuity rate? Is the gratuity taxed?

What other charges might be considered (minimums, overtime, setup)?

What time can you start setting up for your function?

What time do waitpersons arrive - prior to function starting time
    (especially for breakfasts)?

Are there signs for reserved tables, non-smoking and smoking sections?

Can tables be set for eight? Ten?

What linen colors are available? What table decorations are available
    at no charge?

Is it possible to tour the kitchen? Meet the chef?

Are lights and temperature controls in the meeting/dining room able
    to be controlled individually?

Are facilities available for the handicapped?

What audio/visual aids are available at no charge?

What other conventions or groups will be meeting at the same time?

SOME WAYS TO REDUCE LIQUOR AND MEAL COSTS:

* Allow no free pouring. Instruct bartenders to use jiggers or pouring measurers, use smaller glasses for drinks, and make sure of the serving size of the drinks.

* Arrange cash bars or fixed cost bars (a cost per person for drinks for an hour). Note that for meetings of under 100 people the least expensive bar is usually priced by the drink, for meetings of over 100 people it is better to price by the bottle.

* Inventory the bar before and after. Have the bartender sign the inventory sheet at the end of the party.

* Use continental breakfasts and hors d'oeuvres rather than sit-down meals.

* Work with the catering staff, advising them of your budget. Have them outline three possibilities to choose from.

* Reduce entree size portions. Use lunch size portions at dinners.

* Schedule fewer coffee breaks and save the dessert from lunch for an afternoon coffee break.

* Utilize ticket systems.

* Use waitpersons to serve hors d'oeuvres.

* Use small plates or don't provide plates at all; use napkins instead.

* Offer sponsorship to companies for offsetting the costs of coffee breaks, cocktail parties, and meals.

* Avoid salty foods during cocktail party events.

* Keep records and instruct personnel that unless extended by you or the designated leader, the events are to end at the scheduled time.

IF AN INTERNATIONAL MEETING IS PLANNED...

Consider local practices and customs. Find out the holidays (local, national, religious, governmental), dress codes, appropriate gifts, local and labor laws, lifestyle patterns, and what is customary such as dining times, tipping, seating order, proper introductions and addressing, etc. Obtain destination brochures and maps, find out documentary requirements, currency information, medical situations, transportation details, security precautions, and other services. Make sure insurance coverages are in order. Hire translation services if necessary.

SOME HINTS ABOUT TIPPING...

The following guidelines are provided primarily for U.S. hotels and resorts, since tipping in some countries is not customary.

Bellpersons - $1.00 per bag when they show you to the room and also upon check out if they take your bags down. Extra may be given if you have excess baggage or materials.

Concierge - Tip when special services have been rendered such as reservations made, theater or sightseeing tickets obtained, etc. $2.00 - $10.00 per service - depending on how involved the service is, or in a lump sum upon arrival or departure.

Doorpersons - No need to tip unless they carry luggage, shelter you with an umbrella, obtain taxis, or other services (then $1.00 or more is customary).

Housekeeper/Maid - $1.00 per night is customary and more if special services have been required.

Parking Attendants - $1.00 - $3.00, depending on the city.

Room Service - 15% of the bill.

Waitpersons - 15% of the bill, an extra 5% if service was outstanding.

Bartender - 15% of the tab is customary.

Busboy - No tipping is necessary.

Maitre d' - $2.00 to $5.00 for special arrangements, $10.00 - $50.00 for leaving a lasting impression and getting the "impossible" table on a busy night.

Musicians - $1.00 - $5.00, depending on special requests.

Washroom Attendants - $.50 - $1.00 is customary.

Cloakroom Attendants - $1.00 if there has not been a charge. A tip is not necessary if there is a charge.

Copyright Claudine Dervaes

REVIEW ON MEETING PLANNING

1. The first step in meeting planning is to _____

_____ .

2. What are three things to consider when selecting a site?

    a. _____

    b. _____

    c. _____

3. Name four contact people at hotels that work with meeting planners.

    a. _____

    b. _____

    c. _____

    d. _____

4. Name three items that are used to promote meetings.

    a. _____

    b. _____

    c. _____

5. As a general rule, there should be at least one staff member for

every _____ attendees.

INVOICES STATIONERY NOTICES

MEMOS CARDS

BUSINESS COMMUNICATIONS

To effectively communicate with suppliers and clients, travel agents use forms and write letters. Correspondence may concern a request, a complaint, an enclosure of brochures, a refund request, an outline of an itinerary, etc.

Some of the standard forms include stationery, invoices, thank you notes, and reservation/confirmation forms. The following pages provide samples of many forms. Designs and formats may vary from agency to agency. All forms, names and logos shown are for example purpose only.

Business writing skills, formats and sample business letters are also provided. Any similarity of names, places, and situations is purely coincidental.

Business communications can refer to telephone and sales techniques, reporting and management procedures, in-house communications and the ability to use resources. Since telephone and sales techniques have already been covered, this part will cover some accessory areas such as: correspondence to airlines, agency management forms, and travel agency filing procedures.

LETTERS REPORTS

RESERVATION FORMS FILES

EVALUATIONS

BUSINESS COMMUNICATIONS

A travel agency will have a supply of printed materials for its business communications. These items should project a professional and appealing image. Colored paper and colored ink can enhance appearance. Office communication supplies include:

> Letterhead Stationery
> Envelopes (window and plain)
> Business Cards
> Invoices
> Itinerary Forms
> Vouchers
> Memos

Most of these forms can be supplied on computer paper so they can be printed by using the computer/word processing equipment in the agency.

STATIONERY, BUSINESS CARD, AND MEMO SAMPLE

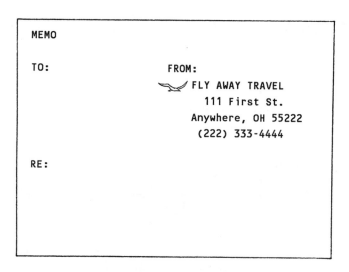

*Use your logo on
all stationery items.*

SAMPLE INVOICE/ITINERARY FORM

FLY AWAY TRAVEL
111 First St.
Anywhere, OH 55222
(222) 333-4444

NO. 123456

TO:

Agent	Contact	Customer #	Account #	Date

Code	Day	Date	City/Arpt.	Time	Carrier	Flt#,Class	Amount

CODES: A - AIR H - HOTEL C - CAR T - TOUR S - SURFACE
W - CRUISE V - OTHER TRAVEL SERVICE

STATUS CODES: OK - CONFIRMED RQ - REQUESTED WL - WAIT LIST

OTHER SAMPLE FORMS

Ticket Jacket/Cover:

 FLY AWAY TRAVEL
            111 First St.
            Anywhere, OH 55222
            (222) 333-4444

TICKETS FOR:

Please call us for your airline, hotel, car rental, tour, cruise,
reservations; vacation or business travel; group or specialty tours!

On the back of the cover:

Thank you for using Fly Away Travel for your travel plans. Remember to reconfirm
your reservations directly with the airline, check in at least 1 hour prior for
domestic flights and 2 hours prior for international flights. Check over your
documents when you receive them. If you must change your itinerary, additional
costs may be involved. Guard your ticket! Lost, stolen, or destroyed tickets
cannot be refunded unless and until authority has been granted by the airline,
and with an imposed service charge. Because of the possibility of an airline
default or bankruptcy of a carrier or other supplier, we highly recommend the
purchase of insurance. This travel agency is acting as an intermediary for the
suppliers or services and is therefore not responsible for breach of contract or
negligence on the part of those suppliers. This travel agency hereby gives notice that it cannot be responsible for disruption of travel, damages, or injury
that results from terrorist acts, monetary crisis, political or social unrest,
labor problems, mechanical or other difficulties, local laws, health or climate
conditions, or outbreaks of disease.

Payment Past Due Notice:

Date:_____
RE: Invoice #_____
Invoice dated_____
Amount due_____

TO:

FROM: Fly Away Travel
             111 First St.
             Anywhere, OH 55222
             (222) 333-4444

JUST A REMINDER: If the payment
has already been mailed, thank you!
If you have not paid the amount
due, please respond immediately to
this notice to hold your reservations.

120

SAMPLE ENCLOSURE OF BROCHURES FORM

```
FROM:        FLY AWAY TRAVEL        THANK YOU FOR YOUR INQUIRY!
             1111 First St.         We have enclosed flyers or brochures
             Anywhere, Oh 44555     that pertain to your travel plans
             (222) 333-4444         and needs. Please contact us if you
                                    have any questions and remember that
                                    reservations should be made as early
TO:                                 as possible.


                                    AGENT_____
```

CORRESPONDENCE WITH VENDOR FORM

```
DATE:_____
FROM:        FLY AWAY TRAVEL        RE CLIENTS:_____
             1111 First St.         TOUR/SHIP NAME_____
             Anywhere, Oh 44555     DEPARTURE DATE:_____
             (222) 333-4444         IT#(if applicable)_____
                                    __Deposit of_____enclosed
                                    __Final payment of_____enclosed
TO:                                 CHECK #_____
                                    CREDIT CARD#_____
                                    __Please cancel reservations
                                    __Refund the amount of_____

MESSAGE_____
_____
_____
                                    AGENT_____
```

SAMPLE ITINERARY FORM

ITINERARY PREPARED FOR:_____				BY: FLY AWAY TRAVEL (222) 333-4444			
DAY	DATE	AIRLINE,FLT.#	DEPART CITY	TIME	ARRIVE CITY	TIME	MEALS/ STOPS

In addition to the forms shown, agencies can design forms or order helpful brochures and pamphlets to provide information to the client, such as "Helpful Information About Your Tour," "Questions and Answers about Cruises," "Traveling Safely," "Know Before You Go," etc. Flyers, brochures, and pamphlets are available from many sources: individual tour companies and cruise lines, Cruise Lines International Association (CLIA), American Society of Travel Agents (ASTA), Travel Professionals Association, Inc. (TPA), U.S. Customs, etc.

Below is a TRAVEL CHECKLIST that is available in quantities from the Travel Professionals Association, Inc. for handing out to clients in preparation for their trip.

```
TRAVEL CHECKLIST
___suitcase, carry-on, garment bag
___wallet, cash, travelers checks
___passport, I.D., driver's license
___visa, proof of citizenship, shots
___airline ticket, vouchers, tickets
___credit cards, Int'l Driving Lic.
___maps, language books, guidebooks
PERSONAL ITEMS ___soap ___shampoo
___toothbrush & toothpaste ___brush
___razor ___medicines/prescriptions
___lotion ___first aid ___hair dryer
___wash cloth ___toilet paper/tissue
___birth control ___sewing kit/pins
OTHER_____
CLOTHING ___slacks ___shirts ___ties
___dresses/skirts ___jackets ___socks
___shorts ___underwear ___stockings
___walking shoes ___dress shoes
___swimsuit ___sweater ___gloves
___sleepwear ___slip ___belts ___hat
OTHER_____
USEFUL ITEMS ___pocket knife
___alarm clock ___watch ___books
___cards ___camera & film ___adapter
___insect repellent ___binoculars
___tennis racket/balls ___mask/fins
___candle/flashlight ___clothesline
___laundry/souvenirs bag ___snacks
___water bottle ___umbrella/raincoat
___magazines ___sunglasses,sunscreen
___stationery,stamps(if appl.) ___pen
USEFUL INFORMATION:
___stop newspaper
___stop mail
___pets in kennel
___advise neighbor to watch house
___leave key with relative, neighbor
___turn off air conditioner
___turn off water heater
___unplug major appliances
___put extra jewelry, valuables in
   safety deposit box
___pay bills that will be due
        AGENCY STAMP
```

Copyright Claudine Dervaes

BUSINESS WRITING SKILLS

1. Be sure to provide all the FACTS & DATA:

    a. Names of clients

    b. Dates

    c. Name of tour/cruise ship, IT* number (if applicable), etc.

    d. Exact details if correspondence involves a complaint or problem.

2. Enclose receipts, invoice copies, vouchers, and keep a copy for your files.

3. Try to limit letters to one page, and write short, clear, and concise sentences.

4. Avoid trite words and phrases like "Enclosed please find," "we are in receipt of," "the undersigned," "beg," "hereto," "herewith," "in the amount of," etc. Just say "Enclosed is," "we received," and other short and simple words.

5. Use active sentences such as "Please mail a deposit of $100.00 by April 10," NOT "It is requested that you mail a deposit of $100.00 by April 10."

6. State what type of compensation is desired, if known.

7. Write professionally and without anger or crude comments.

8. Send a copy or get approval from your clients if you are writing on their behalf.

9. If the situation is too subjective, have your clients write instead of you. Indicate that you will be glad to follow up with a phone call to check on the complaint being processed.

10. Follow up on letters and complaints accordingly.

*Inclusive Tour

PARTS OF A BUSINESS LETTER

1. LETTERHEAD
2. DATE LINE
3. INSIDE ADDRESS
4. SALUTATION
5. BODY

6. COMPLIMENTARY CLOSE
7. SIGNATURE
8. TYPED NAME AND TITLE
9. INITIALS OF PERSON/TYPIST
10. ENCLOSURE (if applicable)

(1) XYZ Travel
1111 Main Street
Youngstown, OH 55555

(2) Month 00, Year

(3) Casablanca Tours
1555 Zebra Court
New York, NY 11111

(4) Dear Sir:

(5) XXXXXXXXXXXXXXXXXXXXXXXXXXXXXXXXXXXXXXXXXXXXXXXXXXXXXXXXXXXXXXXXXXXXXXXX
XXXXXXXXXXXXXXXXXXXXXXXXXXXXXXXXXXXXXXXXXXXXXXXXXXXXXXXXXXXXXXXXXXXXXXXXXX
XXXXXXXXXXXXXXXXXXXXXXXXXXXXXXXXXXXXXXXXXXXXXXXXXXXXXXXXXXXXXXXXXXXXXXXXXX
XXXXXXXXXXXXXXXXXXXXXXXXXXXXXXXXXXXXXXXXXXXXXXXXXXXXXXXXXXXXXXXXXXXXXXXXXX
XXXXXXXXXXXXXXXXXXXXXXXXXXXXXXXXXXXXXXXXXXXXXXXXXXXXXXXXXXXXXXXXXXXXXXXXXX
XXXXXXXXXXXXXXXXXXXXXXXXXXXXXXXXXXXXXXXXXXXXXXXXXXXXXXXXXXXXXXXXXXXXXXXXX.

XXXXXXXXXXXXXXXXXXXXXXXXXXXXXXXXXXXXXXXXXXXXXXXXXXXXXXXXXXXXXXXXXXXXXXXX
XXXXXXXXXXXXXXXXXXXXXXXXXXXXXXXXXXXXXXXXXXXXXXXXXXXXXXXXXXXXXXXXXXXXXXXXXX
XXXXXXXXXXXXXXXXXXXXXXXXXXXXXXXXXXXXXXXXXXXXXXXXXXXXXXXXXXXXXXXXXXXXXXXXX.

(6) Sincerely yours,

(7) *Timothy Travel*

(8) Timothy Travel
Travel Agent

(9) TT/cd

(10) Enclosure

124

FULL BLOCK FORMAT

FLY AWAY TRAVEL
1111 First Street
Anywhere, OH 55222
(222) 333-4444

May 20, 199_

French National Tourist Office
121 North 54th Avenue
New York, New York 11565

Dear Sir or Madam:

I am writing to request any information that you may have pertaining to castle accommodations in your country. I am interested in details concerning locations, facilities available, costs, and reservation requirements in addition to any other pertinent information.

I have a client who is very interested in this type of vacation.

Any assistance you can provide will be greatly appreciated. Thanking you in advance for your prompt attention to this matter.

Yours truly,

Janna Erwin

Janna Erwin
Travel Agent

In the FULL BLOCK FORMAT, a left-hand margin is used without any indentations for the body of the letter.

MODIFIED BLOCK FORMAT

FLY AWAY TRAVEL
1111 First Street
Anywhere, OH 55222
(222) 333-4444

March 20, 199_

Ms. Polly Polka
9845 Santa Rose Place
Tampa, Florida 33624

Dear Ms. Polka:

Thank you for your letter requesting information on seven night Caribbean cruises. We are pleased to enclose brochures from a number of attractive ships.

I am also enclosing a brochure with general information about cruising as well as practical information about what to wear.

I will be happy to help you choose which ship best serves your needs. To insure the best choice of cabin, we suggest arrangements be made at least six months in advance.

Once again, thank you for your inquiry. We look forward to being of service to you.

Sincerely,

Angie Agent

Angie Agent
Travel Counselor

Enclosures

In the **MODIFIED BLOCK FORMAT**, the date and closing are in line on the right. The body of the letter is indented from the left-hand margin.

BUSINESS LETTERS EXERCISE

For practice, type letters for the following situations:

If a typewriter is unavailable, write neatly on blank paper, using appropriate business letter formats.

NOTE: For company or tourist office addresses, use available reference books or make up addresses. Names and situations are for example only.

1. Write the Belgian National Tourist Office to ask for campground information. Your clients are particularly interested in camping in the Ardennes region.

2. Write to American Airlines on behalf of your clients who were involuntarily bumped from their flight (AA 123, Sep. 10, Paris to Raleigh/Durham). They had to overnight at a hotel and they need to be reimbursed for the cost (receipt from hotel will be enclosed).

3. Write to the Vermont Tourist Information Office to ask about ski resorts, transportation, accommodations, and other particulars.

4. Write to Shipwreck Cruises to complain on behalf of your clients, Mr. and Mrs. R.A. Pain, who sailed on the S/S Stayafloat, June 5, Cabin 555. Their cabin was not cleaned two of the five days of the cruise. They also had requested vegetarian meals (two months prior to cruise date) and were never given any satisfactory entrees. When they complained, the maitre d' and waiter were rude.

5. Write to Getaway Forever Tours to compliment them on the wonderful tour experienced by your clients, Mr. and Mrs. Ernest Sangley. They were on the Grand Pacific Tour, Sept. 28.

SAMPLE FORM LETTERS

In addition to the computer reservation systems, many travel agencies have computers for word processing, mailing lists, and other functions. Sample form letters can be designed for correspondence regarding debit memos, complaints, marketing and promotional letters, etc. Some examples of letters will be provided here. First, a note about debit memos.

DEBIT MEMOS - When airlines send debit memos to travel agencies it is important to verify the charges due. If there is a mistake with the memo, correspondence should be directed to the airline, enclosing applicable documentation and citing applicable rules and regulations (the ARC Handbook has sections on credit card charge acceptance and other liability concerns).

Since the laws vary from state to state, an agency should consult an attorney before using any forms for correspondence. In addition, Solitaire Publishing is not responsible for any interpretation or use of these sample forms.

SAMPLE RESPONSE TO A DEBIT MEMO

```
                    Getaway Travel
                     888 9th St.
                    Home, IN 65343
                   (222) 333-4444


   April 5, 1999

   Flyaway Airlines
   4545 7th St.
   Anywhere, NJ 54423

   We have received a debit memo (copy attached) for a ticket
   that cannot be verified by the information you have provided.

   Please provide a copy of the ticket or other documents that
   substantiate this claim. We will examine the documents and
   pay in full any valid claim to monies owed. If sufficient
   documentation cannot be provided, we cannot provide payment.

   Thank you for your attention to this matter.


   Sincerely yours,

   Betty Boop
   Betty Boop
   Agency Manager


   cc: J. R. Jorty, Esq.
   attachment
```

SAMPLE RESPONSE TO A RECALL COMMISSION STATEMENT

```
                         Getaway Travel
                          888 9th St.
                         Home, IN 65343
                         (222) 333-4444


May 15, 1999

Flyaway Airlines
4545 7th St.
Anywhere, NJ 54423


We have received a recall commission statement on the sale
of a ticket that was non-refundable. Because of the following
reasons, we must disagree that a recall commission is due:

1. Our client requested from us a refund for this non-refundable
   ticket. In accordance with Flyaway Airline rules, we informed
   the client that a refund was not permitted.

2. The client then went directly to Flyaway Airlines and was
   given a refund in violation of your own rules.

Our agency acted on behalf of Flyaway Airlines in following
your airline rules. Our agency's credibility and usefulness
are questioned when the client can circumvent our efforts to
comply with your airline rules. Under such circumstances, we
do not feel that our commission should be recalled.

A copy of the ticket is attached for your review.

Thank you in advance for your consideration and attention to
this matter.


Sincerely yours,

Carla Carbuncle

Carla Carbuncle
Agency Manager


cc: J. R. Jorty, Esq.
attachment
```

A sample form can be designed to handle a number of different responses in a "checklist" type fashion:

TO: Airline name and address   Date_____

FROM: Agency name and address

RE: ___DEBIT MEMO #_____   ___RECALL COMMISSION

Please refer to the items checked below as to why we cannot respond to
your request for an amount due.

___Insufficient documentation. Please provide us with a copy of the ticket
   (#_____) or other substantiation.

___Conjunction ticket, no monies due. Check previous/following ticket.

___Ticket was auto-priced by CRS. Address debit to_____(CRS).

___Ticket was non-refundable, and therefore commission should not be recalled.

___Ticket was reported in the _____(date) ARC Report (copy attached).

___Split payment transaction, no monies due.

___Transaction is over two years old. According to the ARC Handbook, agents
   are only obligated to keep files of documents for two years. Therefore,
   we cannot verify the debit and cannot pay the amount due.

___Other_____
   _____

**Other items can be included in the "checklist," plus a form for a
response from the airline can accompany the correspondence mailed.**

**Contact the American Society of Travel Agents (ASTA) for their packet
which outlines a number of letters and information regarding debit memos.
In addition, ARTA (Association of Retail Travel Agents), plus consortium
and franchisor groups can assist their members with effective procedures
for handling problems with vendors.**

130

SAMPLE LETTER HANDLING A COMPLAINT

Lifestyles Travel
621 Main St.
Justaround, NH 00000
(888) 999-0000

May 7, 1999

Mr. R. A. Pain
454 Bugaboo Lane
Keepaway, NH 09999

Dear Mr. Pain:

Thank you for making us aware of the problems you had on your recent trip to _____. I can understand how inconveniences like the ones you experienced can make your trip unpleasant.

We will make every effort to ensure this type of misunderstanding does not happen again, and we would like the opportunity to improve and demonstrate our professional services to you for your next travel plans.

Please know that our priorities are in servicing our valued customers and we greatly appreciate being informed if anything is not done correctly or to your utmost satisfaction.

Thank you!

Harriet Harrassed

Harriet Harrassed
Agency Manager

In some complaint cases, there may be a need for the agency to write to a vendor on behalf of the client or to provide some type of compensation for an error on the agency's part.

It is extremely important that complaints be handled satisfactorily and that managers take complaint letters seriously to improve any agency operations or staff deficiencies. The complaints received are only a part of the possible other dissatisfied clients who do not take the time to write or call.

AGENCY COMMUNICATIONS

Since travel agents acquire first-hand knowledge of different travel products on personal, business, or familiarization trips, agencies can use appropriate forms for evaluating these experiences and disseminating the information to the staff. Forms for this purpose include:

    FAM TRIP REPORT
    HOTEL EVALUATION
    CRUISE SHIP EVALUATION
    EVALUATION OF A DESTINATION

There may be other forms designed by agencies.

MANAGEMENT COMMUNICATIONS

Management communications involve monitoring agency services and evaluating employees and job performances. Successful managers have the ability to give quality evaluations and constructive, effective feedback. The right methods of providing feedback increase staff productivity, problem solving, teamwork, professionalism, enthusiasm, and employee loyalty. The wrong methods cause distrust, absenteeism, conflicts, and a constant turnover of employees. When correcting and evaluating agency staff, managers should

> Think about what to say and how to say it
>
> Sit down with the staff member in private for evaluation
>
> Focus on observed behaviors for correction (employee doesn't smile, doesn't use a nice tone of voice, etc.), don't just say the employee "has a bad attitude"
>
> Work with the employee for the necessary changes (ask what may be causing this unpleasant behavior and how it can be worked out)

Evaluations should be periodic and rewards should be given for good job performance. If changes or corrections were in order, there should be a follow-up evaluation. The next pages provide some samples of management communication forms.

FAMILIARIZATION TRIP REPORT

FAM TRIP REPORT by_____DATES OF TRIP_____

FAM SPONSORED BY:_____PRICE(optional)_____

A/L	TKT/GATE SVCS.	INFLIGHT SVCS.	MEALS	EQUIP. MAINT.	BAGGAGE DEL.
___	_____	_____	_____	_____	_____
___	_____	_____	_____	_____	_____
___	_____	_____	_____	_____	_____

OTHER COMMENTS _____
_____

ITINERARY_____
_____

CITY	HOTEL	RATING*	COMMENTS
_____	_____	_____	_____
			_____
			_____
_____	_____	_____	_____
			_____
			_____
_____	_____	_____	_____
			_____
			_____
_____	_____	_____	_____
			_____
			_____
_____	_____	_____	_____

*RATING = 1 to 5 (1 is best): an overall evaluation of the hotel regarding
food, service/maintenance, value for price, decor, amenities, & convenience

TOUR COMPANY:_____ OTHER SUPPLIER(S):_____
GUIDE(S)_____
MEALS_____
SIGHTSEEING_____
OTHER SPECIFICS_____
- -

CRUISE LINE _____ SHIP_____
DATES _____ ITINERARY_____
_____
SIZE/DECOR OF CABINS_____
MEALS_____
ENTERTAINMENT_____
PUBLIC AREAS_____
SERVICES AND CREW_____

EXPLAIN THE KNOWLEDGE YOU HAVE GAINED ON THIS TRIP AS IT RELATES TO SELLING
THE TRAVEL PRODUCTS AND DESTINATIONS INVOLVED:

_____
_____
_____
_____
_____

HOTEL EVALUATION FORM

DATE:_____   COMPLETED BY:_____

HOTEL NAME, CITY, PHONE(S):_____

CHAIN/INDEPENDENT (if chain-identify):_____

BASIC CLASSIFICATION OF HOTEL: ___DELUXE   ___FIRST CLASS   ___STANDARD

LOCATION: ___downtown   ___resort   ___suburb   ___shopping area   ___airport

HOTEL IS MOST LIKELY TO DRAW (check all that apply):   ___couples   ___families

___honeymooners   ___business clients   ___conventions   ___tourists   ___students

THIS HOTEL IS USUALLY FILLED DURING THE   ____WEEK   ____WEEKEND.

BUSIEST MONTHS FOR THIS HOTEL WOULD BE _____

SPECIAL PKGS./RATES:_____

DESCRIBE IN A FEW WORDS THE HOTEL SPECIFICS AND CHARACTERISTICS (if applicable):

HOTEL LOBBY_____

FRONT DESK/CHECK IN/CHECK OUT_____

ROOMS_____

   # of rooms_____   std. room rate_____   deluxe room rate_____

SUITES_____   rates_____

IN ROOM AMENITIES_____

RESTAURANTS/LOUNGES_____
   include:

   ___elegant dining   ___coffee shop   ___bar   ___entertainment   ___dancing

CONFERENCE ROOMS_____

   how many?_____   sizes_____

   meetings coordinator_____

   audio/visual aids_____

___SECRETARIAL SERVICES   ___FAX SVCS.   ___COMPUTER SVCS.   OTHER_____

AMENITIES: ___pool   ___beach   ___spa   ___gym   ___concierge   ___shops
   ___tennis courts - - how many?____   cost_____   lighted?_____   pro shop?____
   ___golf course - # of holes/courses, etc._____
   ___access to a golf course/club:_____
   ___beauty salon   ___tour desk   ___car rental desk   OTHER_____

LANDSCAPE_____

FREQUENT FLYER TIE-INS:_____

REFURBISHMENTS/COMMENTS_____

RATE FROM 1-5 (5 is best):   OVERALL____   CLEANLINESS____   SERVICE____

CRUISE SHIP EVALUATION

DATE:_____   COMPLETED BY:_____

SHIP:_____   CRUISE LINE:_____
RANGE OF RATES_____ LENGTH OF CRUISES_____
CABINS/STATEROOMS   #_____   #_____   #_____   #_____
SIZE OF ROOM   _____   _____   _____   _____
BERTHS (upper/
  lower/sofa, etc.)   _____   _____   _____   _____
FLOOR COVERING   _____   _____   _____   _____
DECOR (rate 1-5
with 5 for best)   _____   _____   _____   _____
DRAWER SPACE   _____
CLOSET SPACE   _____
BATHROOM FACILITIES_____

STANDARD CABIN AMENITIES: ___TV ___RADIO ___REFRIGERATOR ___NIGHT LIGHT
   ___BOTTLE OPENER   ____DRINKABLE WATER ___CLOTHESLINE ___HANGERS
   ___110 V. OUTLET FOR HAIR DRYER ___OUTLET FOR RAZOR ___LARGE MIRROR
   ___WRITING SHELF/DESK   OTHER_____

SUPERIOR CABIN/SUITE AMENITIES: ___TV ___RADIO ___REFRIGERATOR ___NIGHT LIGHT
   ___BOTTLE OPENER   ____DRINKABLE WATER ___CLOTHESLINE ___HANGERS
   ___110 V. OUTLET FOR HAIR DRYER ___OUTLET FOR RAZOR ___LARGE MIRROR
   ___WRITING SHELF/DESK   OTHER_____

RATE THE FOLLOWING WITH A SCORE OF 1 TO 5 (5 IS BEST) AND TOTAL EACH AREA:

LOUNGES AND PUBLIC AREAS
Decor____ Cleanliness____ Lighting____ Roominess____ Seating Comfort____
Air Temperature____ Ventilation____ Acceptable Noise Level____ Acoustics____
Dance Areas____ Bar Accessibility____ Waiter Services____ Views____ TOTAL_____

DECK AREAS AND POOL(S)
Deck Size____ Pool Size____ Shaded Areas____ Deck Chairs Comfort____
Deck Chairs Availability____ Deck Surface____ Pool Features____
Cleanliness____ Safety Features____ Towel Service____ Waiter Services____
Acceptable Noise Level____ Entertainment/Games (if applicable)____ TOTAL_____

DINING AREAS
Decor____ Cleanliness____ Lighting____ Roominess____ Seating Comfort____
Air Temperature____ Ventilation____ Acceptable Noise Level____
                                                          TOTAL_____
OF TABLES FOR TWO_____ FOUR_____ SIX_____ EIGHT_____ TWELVE_____

DINING SERVICE
Promptness____ Efficiency____ Courtesy____ Professionalism____   TOTAL_____

FOOD AND BEVERAGES
Quality____ Quantity____ Variety____ Appropriate Temperature____
Presentation____ Wine Selection____ Drinks Selection____
Reasonable Cost For Beverages____ Special Diets Available____   TOTAL_____

ENTERTAINMENT
Quality____ Variety____ Professionalism____   TOTAL_____

PASSAGEWAYS
Width____ Height____ Lighting____ Floor Surface____ Hand Rails____
Ashtrays____ Freedom from obstructions____ Suitable for Handicapped____ TOTAL_____

CABIN SERVICE
Promptness____ Courtesy___ Efficiency____ Professionalism____   TOTAL_____

CRUISE SHIP EVALUATION (continued)

CABIN FOOD SERVICE (Indicate N/A if not applicable)
Prompt____   Presentation____   Appropriate Temperature____   Quality____
Quantity____   Other comments_____   TOTAL_____

THEATRE
Accessible____   Seating Comfort____   Roominess____   View____   Acoustics____
Lighting____   Air Temperature____   Movie Selection____   Program Frequency____
                                                                    TOTAL_____

OTHER FACILITIES (Indicate N/A if not applicable)

SHOPS____   PURSER'S OFFICE____   TOUR DESK____   PHOTO SHOP____   BEAUTY SALON____

CHAPEL____   HOSPITAL____   EXERCISE ROOM____   SAUNA____   CHILDREN'S PLAYROOM____

INDOOR POOL____   STAIRWAYS____   ELEVATOR OPERATIONS____   ELEVATOR AVAILABILITY____

CASINO____   SLOT MACHINES____   FULL CASINO____   CASINO SERVICES____   TOTAL_____

OTHER SERVICES

DANCE/AEROBIC CLASSES____   CRAFT CLASSES____   ORGANIZED GAMES____   LECTURES____

CRUISE DIRECTOR____   EASE OF EMBARKATION____/DEBARKATION____   INFORMATION____

CHILDREN'S ACTIVITIES____   EXCURSIONS/TOURS AT PORTS____   BULLETINS____   TOTAL_____

                                        GRAND TOTAL = _____

TIPPING POLICIES AND PROCEDURES:

_____

BASIC CLASSIFICATION OF SHIP: ___DELUXE   ___FIRST CLASS   ___STANDARD

SHIP IS MOST LIKELY TO DRAW (check all that apply):   ___couples   ___families

___honeymooners   ___business clients   ___singles   ___tourists   ___students

___elderly   ____first time cruisers   ___experienced cruisers   ___adventure seekers

BUSIEST MONTHS FOR THIS SHIP WOULD BE _____

SPECIAL PKGS./RATES:_____

_____

PIER FACILITIES AND SERVICES (rate 1 to 5 with 5 being the best):
Cleanliness____   Air Temperature____   Baggage Handling____   Lighting____
Staff Efficiency____   Parking Facilities____   Roominess____   Seating Comfort____
Customs Inspection Facilities____   Weather Protected____

OTHER COMMENTS:_____

_____

_____

_____

136

EVALUATION OF A DESTINATION

DATE:_____   COMPLETED BY:_____

CITY,STATE or PROVINCE,COUNTRY:_____

LANGUAGES:_____ English widely spoken?_____

APPROXIMATE FLYING TIME_____FROM_____

ROUTING_____

AIRPORT CODE AND NAME_____ Rate 1 to 5 (5 is best):
   Cleanliness____ Appearance____ Baggage Handling____ Staff Efficiency____
   Safety____ Efficient Facility____ Staff Courteous____ Signs Well Posted____

DISTANCE FROM AIRPORT TO DESTINATION_____ TRANSPORTATION AVAILABLE:
   ___rental cars ___train ___bus ___taxi ___subway OTHER_____
Costs of transportation:_____
Advantages/Disadvantages of transportation:_____
_____

NAMES OF SOME HOTELS, THEIR LOCATIONS, PRICE RANGES, COMMENTS:
      (or use hotel evaluation form for thorough details)

_____
_____
_____
_____
_____

OTHER TYPES OF ACCOMMODATIONS (Bed and Breakfast, Campgrounds, Guest Houses, etc.)

_____

NAMES OF RESTAURANTS, LOCATIONS, PRICES, AND COMMENTS:

_____
_____
_____
_____

NAMES OF NIGHTCLUBS, DISCOS, ATTRACTIONS, LOCATIONS, PRICES, AND COMMENTS:

_____
_____
_____
_____

DESCRIBE BEACHES (if applicable):
_____

SHOPPING:
   Best Buys, prices, comments_____
   Local Handicrafts_____
   Best Places To Shop_____
Bargaining Policies_____
   Shops Accept Local Currency____ U.S.Dollars____ Credit Cards____(_____)

SAFETY:
Safe To Walk Around At Night? To Go Alone? Any Special Concerns for Men/Women?
Lock Valuables? Wear Jewelry? Carry A Purse? Park Anywhere? Comments:
_____
_____
Special Hints/Information:_____
Remarks About Visitors/Residents:_____

Copyright Claudine Dervaes

SAMPLE FORM FOR SERVICING COMMERCIAL ACCOUNTS

REPRESENTATIVE_____

DATE_____

COMPANY_____   SPOKE WITH_____

PHONE_____   TITLE_____

ITEMS REVIEWED_____
_____
_____
_____
_____

PROBLEMS_____
_____
_____
_____

VACATION LEADS_____
_____
_____

OTHER REFERRALS_____
_____
_____

FOLLOW UP ITEMS_____
_____
_____
_____
_____

CHECKLIST FOR NEW COMMERCIAL ACCOUNTS

DATES   COMPANY_____ PHONE_____

_____   1. Account representative delivers agency kit and obtains
               profile forms and all pertinent information.

_____   2. Make an appointment to speak to the travel manager/decision
               maker.

_____   3. Go over agency kit with decision maker and invite personnel
               to review agency operations.

_____   4. Appointment for key luncheon and agency management meeting.

_____   5. Welcome to the agency gifts and information on bonuses.

_____   6. Send "thank you" after first booking.

_____   7. Executive Travel Planner kit sent.

_____   8. Account representative delivers travel management reports.

_____   9. Key personnel are contacted for servicing reports.

_____ 10. Agency management informed and policy or operation changes
               enacted.

_____ 11. Follow-up letters, reports done.

_____ 12. Incentive travel prospectus done, and follow up (if appl.).

_____ 13. New programs, benefits, etc.

_____ 14. Continue account retention procedures.

COMPLETED BY_____

The agency would establish the "list" of items according to the various benefits and programs available.

EMPLOYEE EVALUATION

EMPLOYEE NAME_____   DATE HIRED_____

AGENCY MANAGER/EVALUATOR_____

RATING: 5 = OUTSTANDING
          4 = ABOVE AVERAGE
          3 = AVERAGE
          2 = BELOW AVERAGE
          1 = POOR

EVALUATION	DATE	DATE	DATE
PUNCTUALITY			
ATTENDANCE			
APPEARANCE			
ATTITUDE			
FOLLOWS INSTRUCTIONS			
WORKS INDEPENDENTLY			
WORKS COOPERATIVELY			
MAINTAINS WORK AREA AND EQUIPMENT			
MANAGES TIME AND RESOURCES			
SHOWS INITIATIVE			

OTHER COMMENTS_____

_____DATE_____

OTHER COMMENTS_____

_____DATE_____

OTHER COMMENTS_____

Copyright Claudine Dervaes

TRAVEL AGENCY FILES

Travel agencies will have files for

CLIENTS/CUSTOMERS

Reservation cards for records of **airline reservations** are normally filed in a central place so that all agents can access the information. "Active" cards are filed by departure date. "Completed" cards (after clients have departed) are placed in a separate file and alphabetized by the client's last name.

NOTE: In "paperless" agencies, the only record of airline reservations is in the computer data, and the computer reservation systems only keep records of reservations for 24 - 48 hours after departure. Therefore, it is a good idea to have a minimal record of reservations as a backup. For example, slips of paper recording the main items of information can be of assistance if the computer is down or the record is lost.

```
 _____
|                                                 |
|  NAME_____  |
|                                                 |
|  DEPARTURE DATE_____  |
|                                                 |
|  PNR#_____ *  |
|                                                 |
|  AIRLINE_____   |
|                                                 |
|  AGENT_____   |
|_____|
```

*Passenger Name Record Number (also called record locator, booking reference or confirmation number)

Files of information and details on clients' **cruises, packages and tours** that are handled by a specific agent are either in a central file or kept at the individual agent's desk. Standard reservation forms should be used so if another agent has to check on payment details or information, the specifics would be clear to anyone checking the file. A folder is normally used, containing the reservation forms, a copy of the brochure or flyer, invoice/receipt copies, etc. On the inside of the folder cover, the agent may record dates and calls to the client. The tab of the folder will show the name of the client, departure date, and destination, cruise, or tour. Deadlines for deposits and final payments should be put in "tickler" files, as well as on a calendar and in the agent's "queues" in the computer.

```
 /  JOHNSON/MR. & MRS. C.    LAS VEGAS  \
/                             NOV. 15    \
 - - - - - - - - - - - - - - - - - - - - -
```

FILES FOR TRAVEL LITERATURE

Travel agencies provide clients with brochures and other literature pertaining to the trip plans, details, and destinations.

Today's travel product marketing can also involve video presentations using commercial video tapes or video productions on the computer screens. Some computer reservation systems offer this video enhancement for displaying hotel, tour, and cruise information. Agencies can also develop their own video library for client viewing, rentals, and sales.

Although videos have gained tremendous popularity, most agencies also use wall racks or stands for displaying brochures. In addition, filing cabinets are used for storing customer documentation such as passport and visa applications, customs information, general information on destinations, and many other bulletins and forms.

Below is an example of how travel agency files can be organized for brochures and other important literature.

TOURS, followed by
GENERAL INFORMATION
and hotel brochures

CRUISES

TOURS	CRUISES
U.S. subdivided by states and regions, by cities	Continental U.S. HAWAII Inside Passage
CARIBBEAN by group, island, city	BAHAMAS CARIBBEAN
CANADA, MEXICO, CENTRAL AMERICA, SOUTH AMERICA	SOUTH AMERICAN sections for Galapagos Is. Amazon R., Orinoco R.,etc.
EUROPE countries, regions, cities	MEDITERRANEAN BALTIC SCANDINAVIAN
MID.EAST & AFRICA countries, cities	TRANS-ATLANTIC AROUND THE WORLD ORIENT, S. PACIFIC
ASIA & SOUTH PACIFIC same as above	WINDJAMMER YACHT CHARTERS FREIGHTERS
TOURS - alphabetical by TOUR COMPANY	CRUISES - alphabetical by CRUISE LINE

Copyright Claudine Dervaes

General information on countries/destinations may be filed separately from the tour information. Below are some additional topics for files, but agencies may also want to include specialty areas such as overseas car purchase, singles tours, tours for the handicapped, etc.

SPECIAL INTEREST TOURS	OTHER SERVICES AND INFO
SKI VACATIONS by area, region, state, city	U.S. PASSPORT APPLICATIONS, VISA APPS.& TOURIST CARDS by country
HONEYMOONS by area, state, city, type	TOUR OPERATORS INFO by company
SPORTS by type of sport, region, city	CAR RENTAL COMPANIES by company
RAIL TOURS by region, followed by general information, Eurailpass info, other country passes, etc.	MOTORCOACH COMPANIES by company
SPA, HEALTH VACATIONS by region, state, city	HOTEL COMPANIES AND REPRESENTATIVES
SPECIAL EVENT PACKAGES, TOURS by event	CRUISE LINES GENERAL INFORMATION
STUDENT TOURS AND INFORMATION	AIRLINE MEMOS AND BULLETINS
CONDOMINIUM VACATIONS & OTHER SPECIAL INTEREST	CUSTOMS, INSURANCE, TRAVELERS' TIPS

One copy of each brochure should be marked "FILE COPY" and not removed. If the file copy is the only one left, mark it on a "TO ORDER" sheet. A well organized and current supply of literature is a NECESSITY. They are YOUR PRODUCTS, the selling tools that combined with your expertise make your client want to buy. EVERYONE must help in filing brochures.

Agencies also have files or areas designated for stocking the various forms, stationery, accounting reports, extra supplies of brochures, maps, sales and purchasing records, etc. For staff communications, a central bulletin board should post current advertisements and memos (which should also be circulated). Regular morning meetings provide updates, information on fam trip offers, seminars and conferences, etc.

JOB SEARCH AND PREPARATION

After you have completed training and you want to get a job in the
travel industry:

1. Know the area of the industry and specific jobs for which
   you are qualified or that interest you
2. Do your research
3. Prepare your resume and review interview techniques
4. Compile your "job search" chart of progress

More detail on each of these points is given below:

1. Decide whether you want to work for a travel agency, tour company,
   cruise line, airline, car rental firm, hotel or other industry
   supplier. Review your qualifications and the respective job
   requirements. If you're unsure of what you are best qualified
   to do, seek career counseling/planning and use career evaluation
   tests available at local colleges, schools, etc.

2. Prepare a preliminary list of companies and obtain contact names,
   addresses and phone numbers. Use references such as:
      Local newspapers and trade magazines
      Employment agencies
      Local industry associations
      Any contacts/friends already working in the industry
      Listings of companies/associations in resources such as
         The Travel Dictionary, the Travel Industry
         Personnel Directory, membership directories
         of associations, library references such as the
         Encyclopedia of Associations, Occupational
         Outlook Handbook, Dictionary of Occupational
         Titles, Travel Career books and others (listed
         in Books in Print)

   Attend any seminars, classes, conferences, trade shows and trade
   association meetings to pick up information on job possibilities,
   contacts, job search skills, etc.

3. Prepare your resume and interview techniques. There are many
   books available on resume composition, and you may wish to obtain
   additional suggestions from any associates in travel.

   Here are some hints about resumes:
      Write it yourself - look at examples but don't copy them.
      Make every word count - limit it to one page, two at most.
         After a first draft, edit it at least two more times.
      Ask someone qualified to proofread it for errors and grammar.
      Have it typeset or typed professionally and copied on
         good quality paper.
      Stress your accomplishments - no need to be humble on a resume.
      Don't delay - begin with an error-free resume and start the
         job search. If responses seem slow, work on the weekends
         revising it for a better version.

4. See the page on "OTHER JOB TAKING HINTS" for a sample progress chart.

COVER LETTER AND RESUME

The COVER LETTER, which accompanies the resume when applying by mail, should "personalize" the application - catering to the needs of the particular employer. It should give a "personality" and "appeal" to your application so that the employer is eager to read your resume.

Generally, the format of the COVER LETTER is:

Paragraph One: State the purpose and reason for applying (interest, response to an advertisement, placement, lead, research, knowledge of the firm, etc.).

Paragraph Two: Highlight your education or job experience as they relate to the position being sought.

Paragraph Three: Bridge the qualities you have to the firm's needs and goals.

Paragraph Four: Reference the resume (unless it has already been mentioned), request an interview, and relate your eagerness/interest in being contacted (possibly include your phone number).

The content of the cover letter can be standardized somewhat, varying slightly for each prospective employer.

The RESUME is like a data sheet and description of your achievements/ accomplishments. It should provide a "snapshot" of what you have done and what you are like.

PARTS OF A RESUME

1. **Identification** - Name, address, phone.
2. **Career or Job Objective** - If your objectives are too broad or too narrow at this time, this category may be omitted. You may want to state in a sentence or two possible short term and long term goals.
3. **Education** - Beginning with the most recent, show dates, institution, location, course of study, and grade average (if B/3.0 or better). Other formal training programs or educational qualifications can be listed at the end of this category or under another category such as "Additional Qualifications." Depending on the job objective and your individual strengths, this category may either precede or follow the category "Experience."
4. **Experience** - Full and part-time continuous positions extending over a year or more should be listed, beginning with the most recent. For those with many jobs held, indicate the most recent and valued and group together in a statement the several positions which have been held. There is no need to elaborate on positions such as cashier, waitress, bank teller, but include any special responsibil- ities and achievements which may be of interest to the prospective employer.
5. **Additional Qualifications/Travel Related Experiences** - Here is the category to state the areas/countries/cities where you have visited or lived and special skills such as languages spoken, licenses/ certifications, and other non-degree training.

6. **Interests, Hobbies, and Other Activities** - Memberships in honorary, professional and social organizations (in that order) are mentioned here. Community services and other activities plus your hobbies and interests can comprise a second statement in this category.
7. **References** - If you decide to include references provide the full name, position/title, address, and phone number for contact. Make certain your references know that a prospective employer may contact them. You may want to state "References available on request" if you are not sure of the type of references the employer may want.

The cover letter and resume are designed to:

ATTRACT attention

   AROUSE interest

      CREATE desire

         CONVINCE judgement

            MOTIVATE action

SAMPLE COVER LETTER

---

123 4th Street
New York, NY 11111
(888) 888-8888

Mr. Jim Johnson
XYZ Travel
444 5th Street
New York, NY 11111

March 12, 1992

Dear Mr. Johnson,

I am seeking a position as a leisure travel agent with your company and have enclosed my resume for your review.

As my resume indicates, I have traveled through much of Europe and have lived in Asia for a period of time. Combined with my language skills, recent travel training, and job experiences, I know that I can assist your agency in acquiring and professionally servicing leisure travel clients. I am also interested in working with groups for tour and cruise travel arrangements.

I look forward to obtaining an interview for a position with your company and can be reached at (888) 888-8888.

Sincerely,
Harry Smith
Harry Smith

SAMPLE RESUME

Harry Smith
123 4th Street
New York, NY 11111
(888) 888-8888

CAREER OBJECTIVE

I would like to work as a leisure travel agent with the possibility
of specializing in group travel.

EDUCATION

January to June 1992   Travel Training Institute of New York City.
650 hours of Travel Training which included: geography,
domestic and international travel and ticketing, hotels,
car rentals, tours, cruises, sales, and 40 hours on a
Sabre computer. An internship at a travel agency was
also included.

June 1990   Island College, Ithaca, NY. Bachelor of Arts Degree in
Marketing.

June 1986   Arthur Gonzalez High School. Graduated with a 3.8 average.

EMPLOYMENT

June 1990 - present   The Inn at the River. Reservationist and
Assistant Desk Clerk. Voted Employee of the Month six
times.

July 1987 - May 1990 The Coffee Cup. Cashier and waiter. Assisted
the manager with inventory control and supply. I also
helped prepare and set up for banquet functions.

TRAVEL RELATED EXPERIENCES AND ADDITIONAL QUALIFICATIONS

I have traveled throughout France, Germany, Switzerland, Italy, Spain,
and the United Kingdom. I lived in Japan for five years and traveled
to Hong Kong, Singapore, Philippines, and Malaysia. In addition, I
speak fluent Spanish and French and can type 60 words a minute.

INTERESTS AND HOBBIES

I enjoy reading, many sports, the outdoors and hunting. I am an avid
fisherman and like to travel to unusual places.

REFERENCES

Betty Bloomer, Owner
ABC Travel
222 5th Avenue
New York, NY 11111
(678) 888-9999

Mark Mohannon, Instructor
Travel Training Inst. of NY
234567 8th Avenue
New York, NY 11111
(111) 222-3333

INTERVIEW TECHNIQUES

Now it's time to review your interview techniques in order to prepare for getting the right job.

It is a good idea to look upon each job interview as a "final exam." If you have prepared for it, you will do well and it will not be difficult. In order to prepare, review these initial tips:

1. Be sure to know the address, how to get there, and the name of the person you are to meet.

2. Arrive 10-15 minutes early to get a proper feel for the atmosphere.

3. Don't be intimidated. Although it may be viewed as a "final exam," an interview is really a conversation between you and a possible employer. You have the opportunity to find out if it is the right job for you and the employer is finding out whether you are the right person for the job.

4. Be prepared. Have your resume, know something about the company and what you have to offer an employer. Be ready to ask a few questions about the company to show you have a sincere interest.

5. Bring a pen, a small notepad, and have available any personal data (social security card, etc.).

6. Don't bring along any friends or family members.

7. Don't smoke, eat, or chew gum.

8. Dress conservatively. A few rules for men are: Wear a clean, neat, pressed business suit and tie. Have your hair cut and neatly groomed. Be showered, brush your teeth, shave and wear a small amount of cologne or talc if necessary. Trim and clean your fingernails, shine your shoes, and don't wear gaudy ornaments such as gold chains, large rings, and flashy watches. For women: Wear a dress or suit that is in good taste, hose, sensible shoes, conservative jewelry, light makeup and subtle perfume. Be clean, brush your teeth, and have your hair neatly styled. Do not wear gaudy lipstick or nail polish and make sure your nails are clean and not excessive in length.

9. Practice with an associate, friend, or in front of the mirror.

10. Use good manners and do not act impatient, annoyed or restless.

11. Smile and speak distinctly. Do not use slang. Answer questions in full and with "yes" or "no" rather than nodding. Don't fidget or tap your feet/hands. Try not to be nervous, and imagine that you are going to be talking to a friend.

12. If the interviewer offers to shake hands, do so with a firm, steady grip. Do not sit down until you are asked to do so.

13. Look directly at the interviewer; and if the interview includes more than one person, position your chair so you can maintain eye contact with both people without turning your head to each side.

14. When seated, try to sit comfortably and erect.

15. Never criticize former employers. Never beg for a job. Never discuss personal problems.

16. Answer questions truthfully. Don't exaggerate your accomplishments, but stress your strong points.

17. Indicate a preference for the job desired. Don't say you'll take "anything" or you "just need a job."

18. Show an interest in the job being applied for, be able to relate your qualifications, and volunteer important information.

19. Thank the interviewer and leave promptly when the interview ends.

20. Write a follow-up letter or a thank you note for the interview.

QUESTIONS INTERVIEWERS ASK

Here is a list of questions that interviewers ask. Review each question - thinking of how you would respond.

Personal
Do you get along with others?
Tell me about yourself.
What do you view as your strong points? Weaknesses?
Which aspect of your personality would you like to change?
How often were you absent from school or work last year?

Educational
Do you plan on continuing your education?
What course subjects did you like most? Least?

Vocational
Why do you want to work here?
Why should I hire you?
What interests you most about this position?
What are your professional goals?
What did you like best about your previous job?
What did you like least about your previous job?
Why did you leave your last job?
Are you willing to relocate?
What would you like to be doing five years from now? Ten years?
Why did you choose this company?
How long will you stay with the company?
Why have you changed jobs so frequently?
Why aren't you earning more at your age?
What kind of experience do you have for this job?
How would you handle an irate customer?
Do you prefer to work on your own or with supervision?
What salary do you expect?
When can you begin work?
Do you have any references?

Below are some GOOD answers for some of the questions:

What do you view as your strong points? Weaknesses?	I am very honest and hard-working. I need to work on being more patient.
Why should I hire you?	I feel that your company offers me an opportunity and that I can help your operations improve.
Why did you leave your last job?	I felt that my career goals would be better suited in another industry.
What kind of experience do you have for this job?	As my resume indicates, I have held positions in servicing the public. In addition, I have just completed travel training studies and am eager to put my skills to work.
How long will you stay with the company?	As long as I continue to learn and achieve growth potential.
Why have you changed jobs so frequently?	During that time I was interested in participating in a variety of jobs and environments.
Do you prefer to work on your own or with supervision?	At first, I would prefer to work with a supervisor in order to maximize my job skills and understanding.
Are you willing to relocate?	At present, my preference is to remain in the local area, but I would consider a transfer opportunity for job advancement.
How would you handle an irate customer?	First, I would remain calm and try to assure the customer that I want to assist him/her. I would determine the facts of the situation, resolve it, or refer it to the appropriate party.

If you are offered the job during the interview, be sure to thank the interviewer and state that you will do your best in the position. If you are unsure about accepting the job, ask the interviewer if you can call him/her in a day or two with your answer. If you receive a letter from the employer offering the job, contact the employer to accept it, to let him/her know that you have taken another job, or that you are sorry but that you are no longer interested in the position. Write a thank you.

INTERVIEW CHECKLIST

For the INTERVIEWER as well as the prospective employee, here is a sample checklist, with 1 being the lowest and 5 being the highest.

DATE_____

NAME_____

POSITION_____

Other_____

PHONE NUMBER_____

Salary range_____

Salary req'd_____

Score

_____ APPEARANCE
1 Sloppy, indifferent, untidy
2 Careless, poor grooming
3 Functional attire, neat
4 Well groomed
5 Immaculate attire and grooming

_____ ATTITUDE AND POSITION
1 No confidence, lacks direction, very poor posture
2 Appears uncertain, slouches
3 Holds self well, appears confident
4 Very confident, self-directed and motivated
5 Highly confident, inspires others, asserts presence

_____ EXPRESSION
1 Uncommunicative, confused, poor vocabulary
2 Poor speaker, hazy thoughts and ideas
3 Speaks well, expresses ideas adequately
4 Thinks and speaks clearly, confidently
5 Exceptional, speaks clearly, concisely, ideas well thought out

_____ JOB KNOWLEDGE
1 None as it pertains to this position
2 Will need considerable training and supervision
3 Has basic skills, but needs additional training
4 Well trained, very little supervision needed
5 Extremely well trained, no supervision needed

_____ MOTIVATION
1 Apathetic, indifferent, disinterested, no motivation
2 Little interest, doubtful
3 Sincere desire to work and do well
4 Strong interest and desire, motivated
5 Highly motivated, eager to work well, positive

_____ PERSONALITY
1 Unpleasant
2 Slightly objectional
3 Likeable
4 Pleasing
5 Extremely pleasant, charming, very likeable

_____ OVERALL IMPRESSION
1 Unsatisfactory
2 Marginal
3 Satisfactory
4 Very good
5 Excellent

_____ TOTAL

Additional comments_____

Hired? _____YES _____NO   Interview again? _____YES _____NO

The initial steps in your job search should include:

> Knowing Your Skills
> Having a Clear Job Objective
> Knowing Where and How to Look
> Spending at Least 25 Hours a Week
> Getting at Least Two Interviews a Day
> Following Up on All Contacts

A follow-up letter

* thanks the interviewer for talking with you
* tells the interviewer that you are interested
* lets the interviewer know that you think you are qualified for the job

The employer will appreciate your thoughtfulness and you may even get the job because of your follow-up letter.

SAMPLE THANK YOU LETTER

```
                                      774 1st Avenue
                                      New York, NY 11111
                                      May 1, 1999

Mr. John Smith
XYZ Corporation
12345 6th Avenue
New York, NY 11111

Dear Mr. Smith:

    Thank you for taking the time to talk with me on Friday. The
position of travel agent-leisure sales that we discussed interested
me greatly. I believe that I have the qualifications necessary and
hope that you will consider me for the position.

    I look forward to hearing from you.

                                      Sincerely yours,

                                      Penny Lane
                                      Penny Lane
```

OTHER JOB TAKING HINTS

Salary negotiation may also be involved in the job acceptance process. As the employee, be certain that you will be happy accepting the salary offered, otherwise you'll be dissatisfied in the job right from the start. If the salary is not what you expected/wanted, will a raise or increase be possible within a reasonable amount of time?

Before accepting the job - ask yourself: Is this a job I really want? Is this position well suited for me? Am I clear as to what will be expected of me and my job duties? Do I like the office and staff?

Be careful when asking about job benefits - you may sound greedy when your only questions to the interviewer are "How many fam trips will I get? How much vacation and sick days are allowed?" Instead ask the interviewer: "Can you please outline some of your personnel policies with regard to insurance, vacation, and other specifics?" If you have no prior experience in the particular job, but have just completed school/training and feel you are capable, maybe offer to "work for free" for a day/few days/week in order to exhibit your competence to the employer.

In some cases, such as working as an OUTSIDE SALES TRAVEL AGENT, a contract may be necessary to outline the agreed upon job duties and payments due as you are an INDEPENDENT CONTRACTOR. More detail is covered in the section on OUTSIDE SALES.

In your job search, a CHART can be helpful in tracking your contacts, resumes mailed and other specifics. Below is a sample:

JOB SEARCH - CHART OF PROGRESS

COMPANY	DATE	SPOKE TO	RESULT	FOLLOW-UP	INTERVIEW	FOLLOW-UP
XYZ Travel 111 3rd St. NY NY 11111 222-238-1111	11/2	Mr.Smith (phone)	resume mailed 11/5	11/20 - called- interview 12/3	12/3 - went OK - wrote note	call 12/15
COMMENTS _____						
ABC Corp. 2345 6th St. NY NY 11111 344-555-4545	11/3	Jane Edwards (in person) left resume	called 11/14 no openings	12/20 possible interview 1/5	1/5 - part-time available call 1/7	1/7 - said full-time position needed
COMMENTS _____						

SOME POSITIONS IN TRAVEL:

ENTRY LEVEL	ADVANCED POSITIONS

AIRLINES:

ENTRY LEVEL	ADVANCED POSITIONS
Reservationist	Marketing Director
Ticket Agent	District Sales Representative
Flight Attendant	District Sales Manager
Passenger Service	Regional Sales Manager
Clerical/Secretarial	Director of Group Sales
Operations	Traffic Manager
Accounting	Airport Operations Manager
Maintenance	Automation Sales Manager
	Director of Agency Relations

TOUR COMPANIES:

ENTRY LEVEL	ADVANCED POSITIONS
Receptionist	Sales Representative
Reservationist	Marketing Director
Clerical/Secretarial	Sales Manager
Mail Manager	Operations Supervisor
Accounting	Account Supervisor
Tour Escort/Guide	Tour Director/Manager
Marketing Assistant	Ground Services Manager
	Group Sales Director
	Vice-President - Operations
	President

HOTELS:

ENTRY LEVEL	ADVANCED POSITIONS
Reservationist	Reservations Supervisor
Reception/Desk Staff	Sales Manager
Housekeeping	Operations Manager
Bellpersons	Catering/Banquet Manager
Bell Captain	Marketing Manager
Porters	Meetings Manager
Cashier	Group Sales Manager
Accounting	
Agency Sales Manager	
Night Auditor	
Concierge/Guest Services	
Telephone Operator	
Food Service Staff	
Maitre D'	
Waitpersons	
Wine Stewards	
Bartenders	
Maintenance	

CAR RENTAL COMPANIES:

ENTRY LEVEL	ADVANCED POSITIONS
Reservationist	Reservations Manager
Counter Rental Agents	Station Manager
Drivers	Sales Representatives
Maintenance	Operations Manager
Passenger Service	District Sales Manager
	Regional Sales Manager

TRAVEL AGENCIES:

Receptionist
Ticket Delivery
Clerical
Accounting
Outside Sales
Travel Agent - Domestic
Commercial Travel
   Representative
Group Sales

Travel Agent - International
Agent Supervisor
Office Manager
Director of Accounting
Group Sales Manager
Sales/Operations Manager
Commercial Accounts Supervisor
Incentive Travel Specialist
Meetings Coordinator/Director
Staff Development Director
Vice-President - Operations
Owner

The size of the agency dictates the variety of positions available. Small agencies may have three or four agents, one of which is the manager, and all duties are distributed among them.

CORPORATE TRAVEL:

Travel Manager
Travel Coordinator
Meeting Planner

NOTE: These are not necessarily entry level positions and may require experience.

CRUISE LINES:

Reservationist
Clerical/Secretarial
Accounting
Mail Manager
Passenger Service

Air/Sea Ticketing Manager
Sales Representative
Marketing Director
Sales Manager
Operations Manager
Group Sales Manager
Incentive Sales Manager

ON-BOARD SHIPS:
Casino Operations Staff
Casino Manager
Beautician
Gift Shop Staff
Fitness/Dance Instructor
Entertainer
Cruise Staff/Hostess
Guest Lecturer

Activities Director
Nurse/Doctor
Masseuse/Masseur
Water Sports Instructor
Shore Excursions Director
Childcare/Youth Director
Photographer
Disk Jockey

Some of the on-board positions are handled by concession companies, not the cruise line directly.

Note: Food Service Staff, Waiters, Busboys, and Cabin Stewards are mostly foreign nationals hired by the cruise line.

TRAVEL AND TOURISM OFFICES, CONVENTION AND VISITOR BUREAUS:

Receptionist
Clerical/Secretarial
Accounting

Marketing Director
Public Relations Director
Promotions Director
Research Director

PRACTICAL TIPS FOR THE EMPLOYER

On the other side of the coin,
the EMPLOYER who is HIRING
should do so thoughtfully and
carefully.

Have a clear job description and identify the necessary skills.

Don't waste time talking to the wrong people.

Always ask to see a resume before setting up an interview.

Don't overload yourself - start with the best 5-6 applicants.

Fill out the INTERVIEW CHECKLIST and make notes.

Help make the applicant comfortable by an occasional smile.

Listen carefully and as much as possible.

Check references and ask questions such as:
   Was she/he responsible? Would you consider rehiring him/her?

Send a letter right away to applicants that you do not plan to hire.

Interview applicants a second time and introduce them to other staff
   members whose feedback may be helpful.

When the person is hired, make sure the "first days on the job" are
   filled with managerial assistance and perhaps appoint a "buddy"
   to help the new employee feel welcome and explain the company
   operations and specifics of the job duties.

Continue to monitor and enhance employee progress with six month/
   annual evaluations, incentive programs, and an "open door"
   policy so the employee can feel comfortable coming to you with
   any problems.

Correct errors when they occur, but not in front of others. Explain
   the mistake in a reasonable way so the employee doesn't feel
   completely degraded, but motivated to do better. Empathize.

QUALITIES OF A PROFESSIONAL TRAVEL AGENT

Travel agency managers/owners list the following qualities and skills as most important in their consideration of a prospective employee:

Knowledge of geography and familiarity with destinations

Hands-on computer experience

Research ability and knowledge of fares and specifics

Sales ability, appearance, attitude, accuracy, expediency

THE PROFESSIONAL TRAVEL AGENT IS ONE WHO:

KNOWS
- destinations
- products and services
- current trends
- procedures
- ethical practices
- where to find information
- the competition

IS
- attractive in appearance
- interested, enthusiastic
- motivated, sincere
- honest, accurate
- alert, organized
- service oriented
- professional

DOES
- relate to the client
- determine the client's needs
- practice good sales skills
- exhibit good communication skills
- have a good attitude
- listen effectively
- accept criticism graciously

AND SELLS   his/herself, the products, the agency, and the industry!

MANAGING YOUR TIME

1. MAKE A LIST OF YOUR WORK PROJECTS AND GOALS.

2. LABEL THEM AS SHORT TERM OR LONG TERM.

3. REVIEW AND REVISE THE LIST PERIODICALLY.

4. PLAN YOUR TIME EFFECTIVELY.

5. ANALYZE YOUR TIME, NOTING YOUR SCHEDULED AND UNSCHEDULED ACTIVITIES.

6. DIVIDE SCHEDULED ACTIVITIES INTO CATEGORIES:

    A. EXTREMELY IMPORTANT TASKS
    B. NOT SO IMPORTANT TASKS
    C. ACCESSORY TASKS
    D. LONG RANGE GOALS

7. LOOK FOR WAYS OF ORGANIZING THE ACTIVITIES. USE FORMS TO ORGANIZE INFORMATION. HAVE RESOURCES AND QUICK REFERENCE INFORMATION AVAILABLE.

8. IF POSSIBLE, PREPARE A DAILY TIMETABLE (ALLOWING FOR ANY UNPREDICTABLE WORK THAT MAY BE INVOLVED).

9. DELEGATE TASKS WHENEVER POSSIBLE.

10. DO PROMPTLY THE TASKS THAT YOU LEAST LIKE OR ONES THAT YOU WOULD TEND TO AVOID. DON'T PROCRASTINATE.

WORK ACCORDING TO A PATTERN AND FEEL LESS PRESSURED!

OTHER IMPORTANT POINTS TO TIME MANAGEMENT

1. Get a head start by using the morning hours to prepare for the day.

2. Eat a good breakfast. It can improve both mental and physical abilities. Eat a light lunch and light dinner.

3. Make a list of things to be done. Crossing off items gives a sense of accomplishment and a renewed feeling towards the duties still to complete.

4. Work for clients who will reward your time. Don't get caught up with last minute work that may ultimately take longer.

5. Handle difficult jobs by not thinking about them so much, just jump right in and get the job done.

6. Don't let paperwork overwhelm you. Try to minimize the time required by accomplishing these tasks as early as possible.

7. Take a break. If you continue to work through a lunch hour or break, it often results in mistakes and duplicate work.

8. Think about your own personal goals. Set aside time for these goals so that you can have greater self-confidence and self-worth.

9. Don't waste time. Always have reading material with you to use if you are delayed at an appointment or waiting for someone.

10. Don't set unrealistic goals and reexamine your goals from time to time to make them relevant. You may need to change some short term goals to long term ones, or vice versa.

REWARD YOURSELF WHEN YOU HAVE DONE SOMETHING WELL!

DON'T EXPECT OTHERS TO NOTICE YOUR ACCOMPLISHMENTS!

ULTIMATELY, YOU ARE YOUR OWN BOSS!!

STRESS AND BURNOUT

It is important to realize that time management goes beyond the details and organizing procedures to enable the individual to allocate "work" and "non-work" times. The time set aside for relaxation and leisure pursuits will help reduce stress and burnout.

Stress itself cannot be avoided. It is when stress becomes excessive and coping skills over-taxed that stress becomes a problem. There are many responses to stressful situations and what is stressful to one person is not necessarily stressful to another. Awareness is the first step to handling stress. It doesn't require change or control, it requires receptiveness and acceptance.

Burnout is the result of four forces. It comes from (a) job stress - the pressure for sales, reservations, quotas, etc.; (b) habits - a self-defeating behavior; (c) self-concept - the sense of who we are; and (d) the quality of relationships - if you are burnt out at home you will be burnt out at work. Burnout exhibits itself in three dimensions - in an individual's behavior, attitudes, and feelings.

20 WAYS TO REDUCE STRESS AND BURNOUT

*Identify the items that cause stress

*Anticipate and prepare for those times that you know will be stressful

*Focus on options

*Set goals and make plans

*Accept the things you cannot change

*Focus on a better world - see the "big picture"

*Maintain optimism

*Set yourself up to be successful

*When in doubt confront, when all else fails, try honesty

*Reward yourself

*Value the importance of your work

*Focus on the here and now

*Take a break

*Confide in other people

*Engage in self-analysis

*Remind yourself that you are not the target

*Keep everything in perspective

*Change/break bad habits

*Stay healthy and exercise

*Love yourself - unconditionally

10 WAYS TO GROW, BE HAPPY AND SUCCEED!

1. Love your work or learn to love your work, and commit to a goal of being outstanding in your field. You can feel worthwhile and proud that you have become good at what you do.

2. Know that sacrifices and mistakes/errors are all part of growth. In fact, learning and growth result from failures.

3. Be determined and patient. Be willing to accept a slower pace if that is what it will take to get ahead. Be flexible and resilient - bounce back from any disappointment or criticism.

4. Never stop learning. It is what will make your job and life interesting and enjoyable. Your mind is the most valuable asset you have. Continue to invest in it.

5. Associate with people who are success oriented and who are leaders in your field.

6. Use time wisely. Plan ahead. Make every minute count. Don't think of your day in terms of hours, mornings or afternoons; think of it in terms of minutes. Carry a couple of industry newsletters, magazines, brochures, or other worthwhile reading with you so that if you are delayed at an appointment you can use the time constructively.

7. Be honest and true to yourself and others.

8. Use your creativity. Look for newer, quicker, easier, more enjoyable ways to do things.

9. Treat every client as special and every transaction as if it were a million dollar sale. Empathize and put yourself in the client's position to understand and relate better.

10. Work hard and conduct your life in an ethical, moral, sensible, and professional manner. Success is measured in happiness and you can be happy by living a fulfilled existence.

ANSWER KEY

PAGE 1
1. E
2. D
3. B
4. A
5. C
6. I
7. H
8. F
9. G
10. J

PAGE 2
1. 12:10 am
2. 5:52 pm
3. 1:45 pm
4. 5:32 am
5. 2:21 pm
6. 1012
7. 1220
8. 0915
9. 2045
10. 0620
11. D
12. A
13. E
14. C
15. E
16. B
17. C
18. D
19. A
20. B
21. C
22. A
23. C
24. G
25. H
26. I
27. J
28. A
29. E
30. D
31. C
32. F
33. B

PAGE 3
1. Texas - TX
2. Louisiana - LA
3. Kansas - KS
4. Wisconsin - WI
5. Colorado - CO
6. New Mexico - NM
7. Kentucky - KY
8. North Carolina - NC
9. South Carolina - SC
10. Florida - FL
11. Alabama - AL
12. Virginia - VA
13. Tennessee - TN
14. Arkansas - AR
15. Mississippi - MS
16. Georgia - GA
17. Oklahoma - OK
18. Nebraska - NE
19. Pennsylvania - PA
20. Delaware - DE
21. West Virginia - WV
22. Washington, DC - DC
23. Maine - ME
24. New Hampshire - NH
25. Rhode Island - RI
26. New York - NY
27. Ohio - OH
28. Missouri - MO
29. Arizona - AZ
30. California - CA
31. Wyoming - WY
32. Indiana - IN
33. South Dakota - SD
34. Washington - WA
35. Iowa - IA
36. New Jersey - NJ
37. North Dakota - ND
38. Massachusetts - MA
39. Illinois - IL
40. Maryland - MD
41. Utah - UT
42. Minnesota - MN
43. Michigan - MI
44. Nevada - NV
45. Montana - MT
46. Oregon - OR
47. Idaho - ID
48. Connecticut - CT
49. Vermont - VT
50. Alaska - AK
51. Hawaii - HI

PAGE 4
1. Hawaii
2. Maui
3. Lanai
4. Molokai
5. Oahu
6. Kauai
7. Niihau
8. Hilo
9. Kona
10. Honolulu
11. Lihue
12. Waimea
13. Kahului
14. Kaunakakai
15. Lanai City
16. Kahoolawe
17. Hana
18. Kahuku
19. Lahaina
20. Wailuku

PAGE 5
1. Fairbanks
2. Kotzebue
3. Point Barrow(or Barrow)
4. Kodiak
5. Anchorage
6. Nome
7. Skagway
8. Juneau
9. Ketchikan
10. Sitka

PAGE 6
1. Nova Scotia
2. Prince Edward Island
3. Ontario
4. Manitoba
5. Northwest Territories
6. British Columbia
7. Quebec
8. Saskatchewan
9. New Brunswick
10. Yukon
11. Newfoundland
12. Alberta

PAGE 7
1. Mexico City
2. Acapulco
3. Manzanillo
4. Cabo San Lucas
5. Mazatlan
6. Cozumel
7. Guadalajara
8. Merida
9. La Paz
10. Puerto Vallarta

PAGE 8
1. Panama
2. Mexico
3. Guatemala
4. El Salvador
5. Belize
6. Costa Rica
7. Nicaragua
8. Honduras
9. Caribbean Sea
10. Pacific Ocean

PAGE 9
1. Cuba
2. Jamaica
3. Grand Cayman
4. San Blas Is.
5. Vieques
6. Haiti
7. Dominican Republic
8. Puerto Rico
9. St. Thomas
10. Aruba
11. Curacao
12. Bonaire
13. Trinidad
14. Tobago
15. New Providence Is.
16. Grand Bahama Is.
17. St. Croix
18. St. John
19. St. Martin/St. Maarten
20. Guadeloupe
21. Isla Margarita
22. Grenada
23. St. Vincent
24. St. Lucia
25. Martinique
26. Dominica
27. Marie Galante
28. Montserrat
29. Antigua
30. Barbuda
31. Nevis
32. St. Kitts
33. St. Barthelemy
34. St. Eustatius
35. Anguilla
36. Tortola
37. Crooked Is.
38. Mona
39. Great Inagua Is.
40. Turks & Caicos Is.
41. Little Inagua Is.
42. Mayaguana Is.
43. Acklins Is.
44. Rum Cay
45. San Salvador Is.
46. Cat Is.
47. Long Is.
48. Great Exuma Is.
49. Eleuthera
50. Great Abaco Is.
51. Bimini
52. Andros
53. Isle of Youth or Isle of Pines
54. Roques
55. Orchilla
56. Tortuga
57. Blanquilla
58. Barbados

PAGE 10

1. Colombia
2. Venezuela
3. Bolivia
4. Argentina
5. Uruguay
6. Paraguay
7. Brazil
8. Peru
9. French Guiana
10. Ecuador
11. Guyana
12. Chile
13. Suriname
14. Falkland Is.(or Islas Malvinas)
15. Galapagos Is.

PAGE 11

1. Iceland
2. Scotland
3. England
4. Wales
5. Northern Ireland
6. Ireland
7. Portugal
8. Spain
9. France
10. Belgium
11. Luxembourg
12. Switzerland
13. Liechtenstein
14. Italy
15. San Marino
16. Andorra
17. Yugoslavia
18. Albania
19. Greece
20. Turkey
21. Bulgaria
22. Romania
23. Hungary
24. Austria
25. Germany
26. Czechoslovakia
27. Poland
28. Adriatic Sea
29. Denmark
30. Norway
31. Sweden
32. Finland
33. U.S.S.R.
34. Gibraltar
35. Balearic Is.
36. Corsica
37. Sardinia
38. Sicily
39. Malta
40. Crete
41. Rhodes
42. Monaco
43. Netherlands/Holland
44. Atlantic Ocean
45. North Sea
46. Baltic Sea
47. Mediterranean Sea

PAGE 12

1. Morocco
2. Algeria
3. Tunisia
4. Libya
5. Egypt
6. Western Sahara
7. Mauritania
8. Mali
9. Niger
10. Chad
11. Sudan
12. Ethiopia
13. Somalia
14. Senegal
15. Guinea
16. Burkinafaso
17. Sierra Leone
18. Cote d'Ivoire
19. Ghana
20. Nigeria
21. Cameroon
22. Central African Republic
23. Gabon
24. Congo
25. Zaire
26. Uganda
27. Kenya
28. Tanzania
29. Angola
30. Zambia
31. Mozambique
32. Namibia
33. Botswana
34. Zimbabwe
35. South Africa
36. Madagascar
a. Gambia
b. Guinea-Bissau
c. Liberia
d. Togo
e. Benin
f. Equatorial Guinea
g. Djibouti
h. Rwanda
i. Burundi
j. Seychelles
k. Malawi
l. Madeira Is.
m. Lesotho
n. Swaziland
o. Azores
p. Cabinda
q. Canary Is.

PAGE 13

1. U.S.S.R
2. Turkey
3. Syria
4. Jordan
5. Mongolia
6. China
7. India
8. Oman
9. Japan
10. Afghanistan
11. Sri Lanka
12. Myanmar
13. Bangladesh
14. Nepal
15. Saudi Arabia
16. Lebanon
17. South Korea
18. North Korea
19. Thailand
20. Vietnam
21. Philippines
22. Kampuchea
23. Yemen
24. Israel
25. Malaysia
26. Laos
27. Iraq
28. Kuwait
29. United Arab Emirates
30. Oman (another part)
31. Iran
32. Pakistan
33. Indonesia
34. Taiwan
35. Qatar
36. Bahrain
37. Bhutan
38. Singapore
39. Hong Kong
40. Macau
41. Brunei

PAGE 14

1. Auckland
2. Wellington
3. Christchurch
4. Hobart
5. Melbourne
6. Canberra
7. Sydney
8. Adelaide
9. Brisbane
10. Alice Springs
11. Cairns
12. Darwin
13. Perth
A. Western Australia
B. Northern Territory
C. Queensland
D. South Australia
E. New South Wales
F. Victoria
G. Tasmania

PAGE 15

1. E
2. H
3. J
4. A
5. C
6. G
7. D
8. I
9. F
10. B
11. K
12. N
13. L
14. M
15. R
16. W
17. Y
18. Q
19. V
20. T
21. P
22. U
23. X
24. O
25. S

PAGE 16

26. C
27. E
28. D
29. B
30. A
31. I
32. L
33. K
34. F
35. O
36. N
37. M
38. G
39. H
40. J
41. T
42. P
43. U
44. V
45. R
46. Y
47. X
48. W
49. Q
50. S

PAGE 17

1. H
2. D
3. F
4. B
5. A
6. G
7. I
8. C
9. E
10. J
11. K
12. O
13. N
14. L
15. P
16. M
17. U
18. S
19. R
20. T
21. V
22. Q
23. Y
24. X
25. W

PAGE 18

1. Empire State Bldg., Statue of Liberty, World Trade Center, Central Park, Rockefeller Center, Times Square, etc.
2. Buckingham Palace, Big Ben, Houses of Parliament, Tower of London, Picadilly Circus, Soho, Downing Street, etc.
3. Eiffel Tower, Louvre Museum, Champs d'Elysees, Arc de Triomphe, Latin Quarter, Notre Dame Cathedral, Pantheon, Montmartre, etc.
4. Colosseum, Trevi Fountain, Capitoline Hill, Vatican City, St. Peter's Cathedral, Sistine Chapel, Catacombs, etc.
5. Queen Mary, Spruce Goose, Disneyland, Knott's Berry Farm, Catalina Is., Griffith Park, Hollywood, Old Mission Church, etc.
6. Forbidden City, Tien An Men Square, Great Wall of China, Summer Palace, etc.
7. Ginza District, Emperor's Palace, Diet Building, Meiji Shrine, Ueno Park, Iris Garden, Tokyo Tower, etc.
8. French Quarter, Superdome, Jackson Square, Canal Street, Audubon Zoo, Cafe du Monde, Mississippi River, Cities of the Dead, etc.
9. Fisherman's Wharf, Telegraph Hill, Golden Gate Bridge, Ghirardelli Square, Nob Hill, the Cannery, Lombard Street, Chinatown, etc.
10. Alameda Park, Zocalo, Shrine of Guadeloupe, Chapultepec Park and Castle, Floating Gardens of Xochimilco, Zona Rosa, Palacio des Belles Artes, Aztec Ruins, Museum of Anthropology, National Palace
11. Ipanema and Copacabana beaches, Sugarloaf Mountain, Corcovado Mountain, Candelaria Church, Flamengo Park, etc.
12. Opera House, Harbor Bridge, Taronga Zoo Park, Australian Museum, Bondi and other beaches, Cadman's Cottage, Paddington District, etc.
13. Prado Museum, Royal Palace, Museo Taurino, Retiro Park, etc.
14. Red Square, St. Basil's Cathedral, Kremlin, the subway, Gum and Tsum Department stores, Armory Museum, Gorky Park, Mausoleum, etc.
15. Parthenon, Acropolis, Theatre of Dionysus, Roman Forum, Arch of Hadrian, Apteros Nike, Temple of Zeus, Tower of Winds, etc.

PAGE 19

1. A fare for an online connection, or a fare from origin to destination
2. A flight is involved but no reservations have been made
3. A flight that does not require a change of planes
4. An additional aircraft placed on a schedule
5. A trip that has an arunk or surface segment in it
6. Where the passenger sits and what services he receives
7. The code used to make reservations
8. A deliberate interruption of itinerary, agreed to in advance, more than 4 hours in a city (domestic)
9. A change of planes and airlines
10. The time and place where the passenger changes planes
11. MSY   16. BNA
12. LGA   17. SEA
13. DFW   18. BOS
14. LAX   19. DEN
15. IAD   20. CVG
21. Eastern Standard Time
22. Pacific Daylight Time
23. Central Standard Time
24. Mountain Daylight Time
25. Breakfast   Lunch   Dinner

PAGE 20 - 21

1. European Plan - no meals
2. Continental Plan - Continental breakfast (roll & coffee)
3. Modified American Plan - 2 meals daily (usually breakfast & dinner)
4. Breakfast Plan or Bermuda Plan - breakfast daily
5. American Plan - 3 meals daily
6. Room for one person
7. Room for two people who don't mind sharing a bed
8. Room for two people who want separate beds
9. Room for four people
10. Room for three people
11. Individuals or companies who represent hotel properties for the purpose of reservations (they may have block space or just call in individual reservations)
12. Limited choice - clients get a choice of maybe two or three entrees on a tour
13. Clients get to choose what they want from a menu
14. Any five: Avis, Hertz, National, Budget, Thrifty, Dollar, American International, General, Alamo, Payless
15. Any three: OAG Travel Planners, Official Hotel Guide (formerly OHRG - Official Hotel and Resort Guide); Hotel and Travel Index, Fodor's Guides, Fielding Guides, Michelin Guides, etc.
16. 6 pm
17. Any six: Hyatt, Hilton, Marriott, Sheraton, Holiday Inn, Inter-Continental, Sonesta, Ramada, Best Western, Quality Inn, Four Seasons
18. The location and the facilities will differ (first class will be better)
19. Prepaid vouchers, large cash deposit
20. A package is usually just hotel and transfers, a tour is more inclusive - hotel, transfers, sightseeing, meals, and a guide or escort
21. Any four: Instant companionship, worry-free travel, it may be less expensive, details taken care of, prepaid, it can make a trip more meaningful and less hassled because of having to deal with local languages, customs, and currencies
22. Any three: May not provide enough time on your own to explore, less comfortable because of structured itinerary, no freedom, you may not like the people you travel with
23. Any six: Tauck, American Express, TWA Getaway, Globus Gateway/Cosmos, Caravan, Maupintour, Perillo, Tratalgar, Gray Line, Gogo Tours, etc.
24. Any five: Hotels, transfers, sightseeing, meals, escort or guides, travel bags, maybe taxes and tips, cocktail parties
25. A tour company puts the product together and operates the tour, the product is sold through the travel agencies. The tour company is the wholesaler and the travel agency is the retailer.

PAGE 22

1. 2 photos, birth certificate with seal, application, identification, monies ($42.00 if a first time applicant)
2. A stamp or endorsement in the passport allowing a person to enter a country (usually for a specified time)
3. Medical, flight, baggage, trip cancellation, sometimes airline default protection and weather insurance
4. Hong Kong Dollar - HKD
5. Colombian Peso - COP
6. Bahamian Dollar - BSD
7. Australian Dollar - AUD
8. Japanese Yen - JPY
9. Indian Rupee - INR
10. Mexican Peso - MXP

11. CAI	16. MNL
12. LHR	17. NRT
13. ORY	18. PPT
14. BRU	19. MOW
15. CPH	20. ACA

21. Swissair
22. Japan Air Lines
23. British Airways
24. Cayman Airways
25. Trans World Airlines

PAGE 23

1. A
2. E
3. B
4. C
5. D
6. Retractable fins that extend from the ship to reduce sway and rolling
7. To go aboard ship
8. The place where you leave and enter the ship
9. Any four of these: Prepaid, feeling of glamour, prestige, getting away from it all, lavish food and in great quantities, all inclusive cost, unpack only once, gambling available, relaxing, variety of activities and ports, etc.
10. Any three: Another type of vacation may cost less, some may feel confined, you don't stay in ports very long, motion sickness may be a problem, possible bad weather, alcohol is an additional cost, cruises may not be for everyone
11. Waiter, Busboy, Cabin Steward (at times you may tip the Maitre d' and Wine Steward)
12. Any three: Handle questions and problems, store valuables, provide stamps, ship to shore telephone services, may sell shore excursions
13. Port
14. Starboard
15. Gross Registered Tons (GRT) or tonnage
16. Any five: Bahamas, Caribbean, Amazon River, Nile River, Baltic Sea, Mediterranean Sea, South Pacific, Inside Passage of Alaska, etc.
17. Steamship
18. Turbine Ship, Twin or Turn Screw Ship
19. Motor Vessel
20. Motor Ship

PAGE 24

1. Alitalia
2. Sabena
3. TAP - Air Portugal
4. South African Airways
5. Cathay Pacific
6. Thai International
7. AC
8. TE
9. SQ
10. PR
11. Coach, group (probably 10 people required)
12. Special fare, excursion
13. Special fare, midweek, excursion
14. Coach, low season, excursion, 6M means 6 months
15. First class
16. Business class
17. Special fare, shoulder season, excursion
18. Special fare, high season, excursion
19. Coach, low season, advance purchase,
20. Coach, group inclusive tour (probably 15 people required)
21. A
22. E
23. C
24. D
25. B

PAGE 25

1. "Arrival Unknown" - a surface segment in an itinerary
2. Any five: Puerto Vallarta, Acapulco, Cancun, Cozumel, Ixtapa, Mazatlan, Cabo San Lucas, Manzanillo, etc.
3. Outside cabins have portholes, inside cabins do not
4. Single
5. Triple
6. The location and the facilities
7. 10 years
8. Cruise Lines International Association
9. Any three: Flight, medical, trip cancellation, baggage, airline default protection and sometimes weather insurance
10. An escorted tour means the guide is constantly with the group; a hosted tour means the guide is available at certain times.
11. Foreign Independent Tour/Foreign Independent Travel/ Foreign Independent Traveler
12. Federal Aviation Authority or Administration - responsible for airline, airport, aircraft safety, plus testing and licensing pilots
13. Individuals or companies that represent hotel properties for the purpose of making reservations
14. 5 for direct, usually 8 for connections
15. Grand Bahama Island, New Providence Island, Bimini, Jamaica, St. Thomas, Grand Cayman, Aruba, Martinique, Grenada, Curacao, Trinidad, Tobago, St. Lucia, St. Croix, Puerto Rico, Haiti and the Dominican Republic, St. Kitts, St. Eustatius, St. Martin/ St. Maarten, St. Vincent, St. John, Tortola, Eleuthera, etc.

Copyright Claudine Dervaes

PAGE 26

NOTE: These are just some of the cities to choose from.
1. Paris, Nantes, Nice, Cannes, Marseille, Lyon, Cherbourg, Versailles, Bordeaux, Avignon, Dijon, Rouen, Le Mans, etc.
2. Rome, Milan, Florence, Pisa, Turin, Naples, Livorno, Brindisi
3. Sydney, Perth, Canberra, Alice Springs, Darwin, Cairns, Brisbane, Adelaide, Melbourne, Hobart, etc.
4. Tokyo, Osaka, Hiroshima, Nagasaki, Yokohama, Sapporo, Kyoto, Kobe, Nagoya, Kitakyushu, etc.
5. Rio de Janeiro, Manaus, Brasilia, Sao Paulo, Recife, Fortaleza, Belo Horizonte, Salvador, Natal, Belem, etc.
6. Toronto, Vancouver, Montreal, Halifax, Charlottetown, Ottawa, Quebec, Yellowknife, Saskatoon, Calgary, Edmonton, Winnipeg, Frederickton, Thunder Bay, Sault St. Marie, Victoria
7. London, Stratford-on-Avon, Windsor, Plymouth, Bristol, Brighton, Norwich, Dover, Birmingham, Manchester, Liverpool, Leeds, Northampton, Oxford, Cambridge, Bath, Exeter, Salisbury, etc.
8. Madrid, Toledo, Valencia, Barcelona, Granada, Zaragoza, Segovia, etc. Alicante, Pamploma, Seville, Torremolinos, Malaga,
9. Berlin, Bonn, Frankfurt, Munich, Stuttgart, Heidelberg, Koblenz, Cologne, Mannheim, Dusseldorf, Nurnberg, Hannover, Bremerhaven, Mainz, Baden-Baden, Saarbruken, Wiesbaden, etc.
10. Moscow, Kiev, Leningrad, Odessa, Gorki, Tashkent, Kuybyshev, Tbilisi, Baku, Donetsk, Sverdlovsk, etc.
11. Nassau, Bahamas
12. Nairobi, Kenya
13. London, England/Heathrow
14. Toronto, Ontario, Canada/Pearson Int'l
15. Charlotte, NC
16. Rome, Italy/Da Vinci
17. St. Thomas, U.S. Virgin Islands
18. Tokyo, Japan/Narita
19. Chicago, IL/O'Hare
20. Orlando, FL/McCoy
21. Caracas, Venezuela
22. Hilo, HI
23. Papeete, Tahiti, Society Is., French Polynesia
24. Sydney, Australia
25. Seattle, WA

PAGE 27

1. Costa Rica, Panama, El Salvador, Belize, Honduras, Nicaragua, Guatemala, Mexico (may be included)
2. False
3. Denmark
4. Australia
5. False
6. Any ten: Rome, Paris, Madrid, Brussels, Prague, Bucharest, Berlin, Berne, Luxembourg, Belgrade, Sofia, Ankara, Budapest, Warsaw, Moscow, Oslo, Stockholm, Helsinki, London, Vaduz, Vienna, Lisbon, etc.
7. Any ten: Tauck, American Express, Trafalgar, Golbus Gateway/ Cosmos, GoGo Tours, TWA Getaway, Maupintour, Perillo, Gray Line, American Sightseeing International, Travcoa, Island Holidays, etc.
8. Any five: Carnival, Norwegian Cruise Line, Premier Cruise Line, Princess Cruises, Royal Cruise Line, Royal Caribbean Cruise Line, Cunard Line, Costa Cruises, Fantasy Cruises, Windstar Cruises, Renaissance Cruises, Ocean Cruise Line, Regency Cruises, Commodore Cruise Line, Bermuda Star Line, Dolphin, Holland America/Westours, Seabourn, Sun Line, Windjammer, etc.
9. Any three: Travel Weekly, Travel Trade, Travel Age, Travel Agent, Travel Management Newsletter, Meeting News, Business Travel News, Travellife, Travel Holiday, Travel and Leisure, Conde Nast Traveler, etc.
10. Pacific, Mountain, Central, Eastern
11. Operates everyday except Saturday and Sunday
12. Any five: Sheraton, Hilton, Hyatt, Marriott, Holiday Inn, Best Western, Inter-Continental, Radisson, Sonesta, Four Seasons, Days Inns, etc.
13. A flight that does not require a change of planes.
14. Rate is confirmed and a better room or upgrade may be given on arrival (subject to availability)
15. Any three: Carnivale, Festivale, Mardi Gras, Fantasy, Celebration, Jubilee, Tropicale, Holiday, Sensation (1991)

PAGE 28 - 32

1. Any three: Scandinavian Express International, American Express, Maupintour, Bennett Tours, Crownline, Travellers International, etc.
2. Any three: Celebration, Ecstasy, Britanis, Caribe, Seabreeze, Norway, Seaward, Nordic Prince, Song of America
3. Grammercy's Singleworld
4. Any five: Cozumel, Bonaire, Curacao, Grand Cayman, the Red Sea, off the coast of Belize, Pennekamp State Park in the Florida Keys, U.S. and British Virgin Islands, Palau, Great Barrier Reef, etc.
5. Any three: Avis, Hertz, Kemwel, Europacar, Tilden/National
6. Maupintour, Travcoa
7. Vail, Aspen, Breckenridge, Telluride, Crested Butte, Snowmass
8. Depending on company - about $50.00
9. Toyota Corolla, Ford Escort
10. $250.00 (approximate - subect to change)
11. Arlberg Express Train #469 leaves Paris at 10:40 pm and arrives in Zurich at 7:33 am - first class ticket costs $107.00 (approximately - subject to change)

12. Check your files for yacht charter information. Write or call the Virgin Islands Tourist Information Office, check trade publications and travel guides for information.
13. (800) 223-1234
14. Travcoa, Maupintour
15. Leave New York/Penn Station 2:05 pm, arrive in Chicago 9:29 am the next day. Another schedule is leave New York/Penn Station 7:10 pm and arrive in Chicago 1:03 pm the next day. One way coach ticket $122.00, and a round trip excursion fare ranges from $129.00 - $214.00 (prices subject to change)
16. Any two: Royal Sonesta, St. Louis, Dauphine, Omni
17. OAG North American Travel Planner, computer, map - Milwaukee
18. Pan Am World Guide, travel guides, Dominican Republic Tourist Office - no
19. 41-56 degrees Farenheit - OAG European Travel Planner, travel guides, Pan Am World Guide, computer
20. Eurailtariff, call German Federal Railroad - $60.00
21. OAG North American Travel Planner
22. Official Hotel Guide (formerly OHRG), current travel guides, possibly the Hotel and Travel Index, other hotel guides
23. OAG Worldwide Cruise and Shipline Guide, CLIA Manual, Carnival Cruise Line brochure, OHRG Cruise Directory, Official Steamship Guide, other cruise guides - Italian/Int'l
24. 6 hours difference - The Travel Dictionary, Worldwide OAG, computer, travel guides
25. 37, 584 - OAG Worldwide Cruise and Shipline Guide, OHRG Cruise Directory, Official Steamship Guide, CLIA Manual, other cruise guides, Royal Caribbean Cruise Line brochures
26. Computer, Pan Am Immigration Guide, Canadian Consulate - Proof of citizenship and onward or return ticket
27. OAG Worldwide Cruise and Shipline Guide, OHRG Cruise Directory, Official Steamship Guide, call AAA
28. Specialty Travel Index, Jax Fax Travel Marketing Magazine, Travel World News, travel guides, Peru National Tourist Office
29. (800) 227-4500
30. About 13 or 14 hours, computer, Worldwide OAG, travel guides, call the airlines
31. Colorado River. Maps, atlases, travel guides, AAA Tourbook on Texas
32. Jax Fax Travel Marketing Magazine, Travel World News, local newpaper, trade publications, possibly the Brazil Tourist Office
33. Computer, Travel Industry Personnel Directory, travel guides
34. Pan Am World Guide, travel guides, OAG European Travel Planner - if it is the appropriate edition, Czechoslovakia Tourist Office -CEDOK
35. Historic tour to Tucson, Sedona and Oak Creek Canyon, the Apache Trail, Lake Pleasant Regional Park, North Mountain Park, South Mountain Park, Tombstone, Saguaro National Monument, Slide Rock State Park, Petrified Forest - any five: American Sightseeing International Tariff, Gray Lines Sales Tariff, AAA Tourbook on Arizona, Phoenix Visitor's Bureau, maps, atlases, travel guides, brochures
36. Any three: Computer, current travel guides, newspaper, major banks
37. American Eagle, Northwest Airlink, Trans World Express
38. Yes, call Hertz, use computer
39. Computer, Pan Am Immigration Guide, current travel guides, Polish consulate or tourist office

40. CLIA Manual, OHRG Cruise Directory, cruise line brochures, other cruise guides, call cruise lines
41. Specialty Travel Index, Colorado Tourist office
42. Belgium National Tourist Office, current travel guides
43. Official Hotel Guide, current travel guides, possibly the Hotel and Travel Index and OAG Travel European Planner, French National Tourist Office, some tour companies
44. Specialty Travel Index, French National Tourist Office, brochures
45. Thomas Cook Continental Timetable, Britrail, British Tourist Authority
46. About 5 hours - Thomas Cook Continental Timetable, contact Britrail or the British Tourist Authority
47. AAA Tourbook on Tennessee, brochures, Nashville Visitor's Bureau
48. Brochures, call rental companies, Specialty Travel Index, New Zealand Tourist Office

1. Computer, Pan Am Immigration Guide, OAG Travel Planners, current travel guides
2. North American OAG, Worldwide OAG, current travel guides, Jamaica Tourist office, brochures
3. OAG North American Travel Planner, computer, public library
4. OAG Worldwide Cruise and Shipline Guide, Official Steamship Guide, OHRG Cruise Directory, cruise guides, brochures
5. Specialty Travel Index, brochures, travel guides
6. OAG Worldwide Cruise and Shipline Guide, Ford's Freighter Guide, travel guides
7. Spanish National Tourist Office, travel guides
8. Pan Am Immigration Guide, computer, Czechoslovakia Tourist office, current travel guides
9. Pan Am World Guide, Haiti Tourist office, brochures, current travel guides
10. Thomas Cook Overseas Timetable, travel guides, Japan National Tourist Office
11. Call Budget, computer
12. OAG North American Travel Planner, computer
13. OAG North American Travel Planner, computer
14. Current travel guides, Spanish National Tourist Office
15. OAG European Travel Planner, computer, map, atlas
16. Computer, call Hyatt, Official Hotel Guide (formerly OHRG), Hotel and Travel Index, other guides
17. Map, atlas
18. Eurailtariff, French National Railroad
19. Specialty Travel Index, brochures, current travel guides
20. Computer, call Amtrak, Amtrak schedules
21. Call customs, customs brochures, Hawaii Tourist Office
22. Computer, newspaper, major bank
23. Travel guides, New Orleans Visitor's Bureau, check a calendar for the "Fat Tuesday" before Lent
24. Call major European railroad companies, computer
25. Current travel guides, Zaire Tourist office
26. Official Hotel Guide (formerly OHRG), current and specialty travel guides, British Tourist Authority
27. Department of State advisory bulletins, computer, Dept. of State
28. Travel guides, computer, OAG European Travel Planner
29. Computer, OAG North American Travel Planner, Hotel and Travel Index, Official Hotel Guide
30. Computer, call Hertz

UPDATE! The North American and Worldwide OAGs are now called "Desktop Flight Guides" and the travel planners are called "Business Travel Planners."

5. AIRLINE - Any three of these: Use of national airline vs. U.S. airlines, reputation and service of the airline, most convenient schedules, best fares, discounts, override commissions, upfront monies required, cooperation, possible assistance in promotion, bonuses, etc.

   LAND - Any three of these: Tour company's reputation, service, performance, association memberships, default protection, rates, discounts, override commissions, bonuses, etc.; hotels' locations, amenities, reputation, service, rates, discounts, commissions, bonuses; the restaurants' locations, services, food quality, reputation, cleanliness, prices; trip details such as guides, language abilities and knowledge of groups' specific interest; transportation details such as type of bus, space, large windows, toilet facility, air-conditioned, etc.

1. Commission
2. Commercial travel, group travel, leisure travel, incentive travel, also cruise travel, student travel, adventure travel, etc.
3. Independent contractors or employees
4. Any three: Is under another's control for what is accomplished and as to the details and means by which it is accomplished; can be fired; is furnished with tools, materials, and equipment; is furnished a place to work; is required to comply with instructions as to how, when and where to work; receives training; performs activities which are closely integrated with the claimed employer's business; has a set time to work; has expenses reimbursed; must perform services personally; has an ongoing relationship with the employer, has restraints for working with others now or after being discharged from the current claimed employer
5. Any three: Is engaged in independent employment and controls what is accomplished and how it is accomplished; furnishes the supplies and equipment needed, as well as the place to work; pays any expenses; offers services to other businesses or the public; has the specialized knowledge to do the work; sets the hours for work; may delegate work to his/her own assistants; is paid on a straight commission basis; has the opportunity to make a profit or suffer a loss; must complete the work that has been contracted; pays self-employment taxes

1. Know the objectives
2. Any three: Consider where the attendees will come from, the number of sleeping rooms and meeting rooms you will need, and the amenities the attendees may need or want.
3. Any four: Sales manager, general manager, caterer, meeting facilities manager, food and beverage director, front office manager, reservations manager, housekeeping supervisor, audio/visual technician
4. Any three: Flyers, letters, brochures, press releases
5. 50

1. Any three: Who, When, Where, What Cost
2. Weather, interests, events, travel experiences and expectations
3. Self-knowledge, client knowledge and industry awareness, product knowledge, and presentation knowledge
4. Any six: Travel documentation requirements, transportation to and from the destination, accommodations, other transportation needs, possible sightseeing tours, meals and tipping, taxes, travel insurance and other details
5. Any five: Look at the other person, get rid of distractions, control but don't dominate, ask questions and explain answers, think about what the client is saying, organize by categorizing and outlining, take notes, remember the difference between speaking as opposed to listening, make the client feel that he is making the decisions, be a good listener
6. Any seven: Build a resource library; organize your desk and office; learn from other employees, clients, suppliers, and representatives; read the trade press and subscribe to publications; hold staff meetings; attend seminars and conferences; join associations; watch the news; rent films and videos; read books; enroll in courses; learn a language; go to the library and bookstores
7. Look, speak, listen, and act
8. Any six: Provide a professional service, have the information and product knowledge, develop a "niche" or specialty area, educate the consumer, establish customer loyalty by providing personal services, promote, join industry and other professional organizations, attend conferences, look to the future and keep "two steps ahead"
9. Have a positive attitude, be organized and accurate, and have good communication skills
10. First or second, putting the call on hold, thank you

1. Any three: Kitten closing, pro-con closing, third party closing, today only closing, invitational closing, six times "yes" closing, bottom line closing
2. Any six: Group travel, cruise travel, travel for the handicapped, ski vacations, business travel, honeymoons, religious travel, environmental trips, golf/tennis vacations, budget travel, incentive travel (other types could be mentioned)
3. Statistical information such as age, sex, ethnic background, income, educational level, occupation, religion, status, etc.
4. Market
5. Any eight: Telephone book and yellow pages, trade and consumer publications, newspapers, direct mail, radio, TV, videos, outdoor signs, billboards, electronic advertising, promotions, novelty items, public relations, events

1. Any three: Builds a list of clients, expands the base of possible future travelers, offers a large profit potential, allows the agency to mark up the product, diversifies the products to help in weak periods
2. Any three: Mistakes can be multiplied, everything must be geared for the group, planning is long term, more communication skills are required, necessary organizational skills are multiplied, knowledge of the products has to be more complete
3. Any three: Possibly saves money, can be more comfortable, offers companionship, may be more convenient, and can be more customized
4. Any five: Existing clients with their families, friends, clubs, businesses, organizations; agency employees and their families; friends, organizations; community groups; business and professional groups; health club groups; groups of a specific ethnic background, sports or other interest, school/college, age category, status, etc.

SOLITAIRE PUBLISHING
P.O. BOX 14508
TAMPA, FL 33690-4508
(813) 876-0286 or (800) 226-0286 (U.S.)

Thank you for having purchased the Section Six: General Review and Sales Techniques. If you would like to receive other materials, use the form below or contact us.

- -

I would like to receive:

Section One: Intro to Travel and Geography	$19.95	_____
Section Two: Domestic Travel and Ticketing with Travel Agency Computerization supplement	$29.95	_____
Section Three: Supplemental Sales	$19.95	_____
Section Four: International Travel	$24.95	_____
Section Five: Cruises	$19.95	_____
Section Six: General Review, Sales Techniques, Business Communications	$29.95	_____

The Travel Dictionary. One copy for $13.95,
3 copies are $35.95, 25 copies are $275.00 and
100 copies are $950.00.   _____

ADDITIONAL REFERENCES DISTRIBUTED BY SOLITAIRE PUBLISHING:

Pan Am World Guide	$15.00	_____
Hammond Headline Atlas	$3.95	_____
How to Open Your Own Travel Agency	$39.95	_____
How to Get a Job with a Cruise Line	$12.95	_____
Building Profits Through Group Travel	$45.00	_____
Incentive Travel: The Complete Guide	$45.00	_____
Travel Industry Personnel Directory	$30.00	_____
Travel Agents: From Caravans and Clippers to the Concorde	$25.00	_____
Travel Agency Guide to Business Travel	$35.00	_____

Florida residents please add 6.5% sales tax.   +_____
Shipping charges: Contiguous U.S. Orders to $60.00 add 10%,
over $60.00 add 7%. For AK, HI, and Int'l - add $5.00 for
each item ordered. For quantity orders and other questions,
please contact us.

                                    SHIPPING +_____

                              TOTAL ENCLOSED =_____

Name: _____

School/Company_____

Address: _____

City/State/Zip: _____

Phone: (_____)_____

_____ Please mail me a current catalog on all your publications.